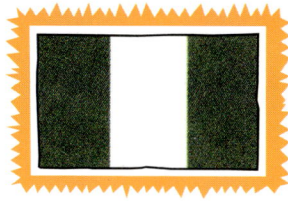

FIESTA!

Nigeria

Tim Cooke

W

FRANKLIN WATTS
NEW YORK•LONDON•SYDNEY

First published 1998

Franklin Watts
96 Leonard Street
London EC2A 4RH

0 7496 2935 5

Dewey Decimal Classification Number: 394.2

A CIP catalogue record for this book is available from the British Library

Copyright © 1997 Marshall Cavendish Limited
119 Wardour Street, London W1V 3TD

Marshall Cavendish Limited
Editorial staff
Editorial Director: Ellen Dupont
Art Director: Joyce Mason
Designer: Trevor Vertigan
Editor: Tessa Paul
Sub-Editors: Susan Janes, Judy Fovargue
Production: Craig Chubb
Editorial Assistant: Lorien Kite

Crafts devised and created by Susan Moxley
Music arrangements by Harry Boteler
Photographs by Bruce Mackie
Consultant: Anthony Adeloye, Chief Librarian, Nigerian High Commission, London

Printed in Italy

Adult supervision advised for all crafts and recipes
particularly those involving sharp instruments and heat.

CONTENTS

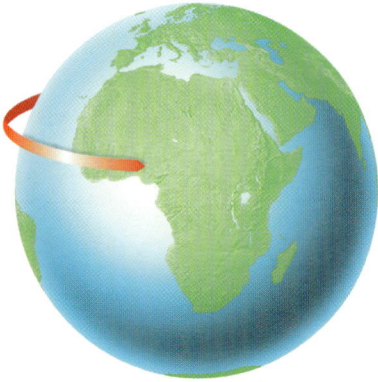

NIGERIA

More people live in Nigeria than in any other country in Africa. Oilfields, mines and forests make it one of the richest countries on the continent.

▼ **Two great religions**, Christianity and Islam, live side by side. A minority of Nigerians follow traditional beliefs.

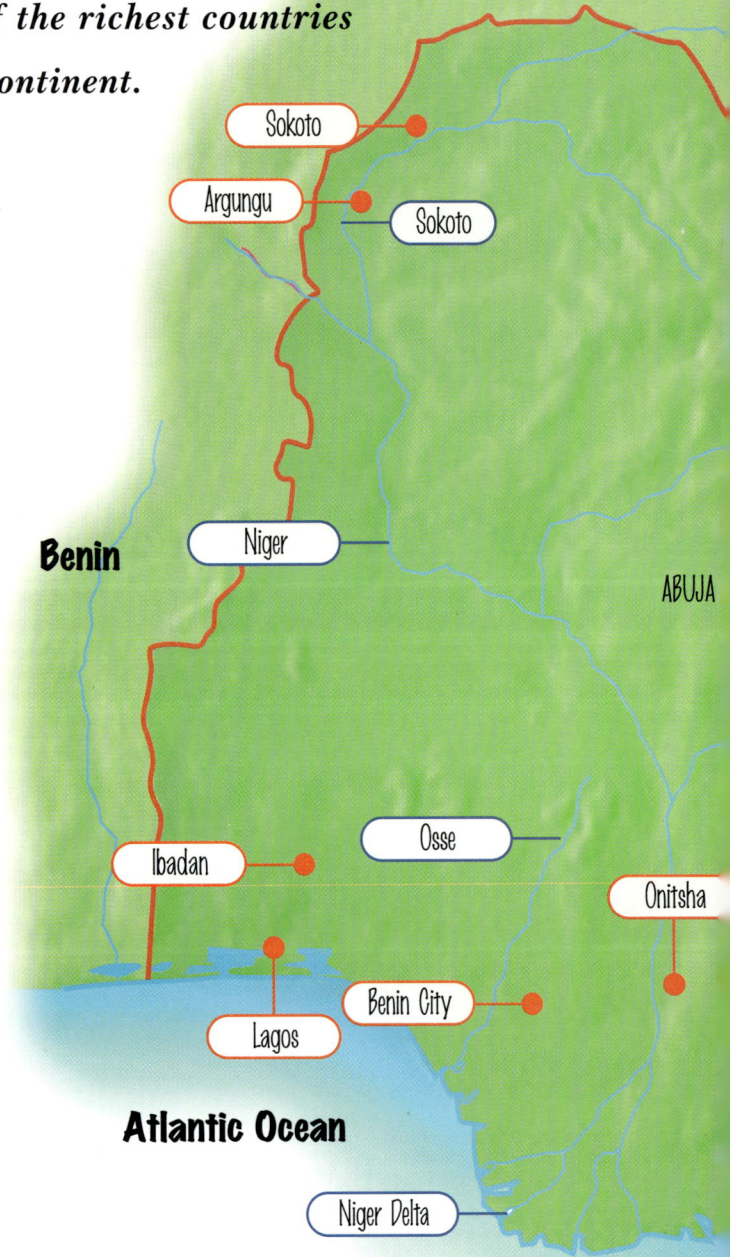

Sokoto

Argungu

Sokoto

Benin

Niger

ABUJA

Osse

Ibadan

Onitsha

Benin City

Lagos

Atlantic Ocean

Niger Delta

◀ **Doma Rock** looms huge and impressive. It is one of many natural wonders in this land. Nigeria has rocky heights, mangrove swamps, rainforests and deserts to explore.

Chad

Lake Chad

Niger

Kano

Maiduguri

▲ **Yams and corn** are pounded into flours in big wooden mortars. These flours are then boiled in water, rolled into dough balls and served at almost all Nigerian meals.

Cameroon

NIGERIA

Benue

▶ **Mud buildings** of great beauty are built in the dry northern areas. This mosque is in Mopti, in the Mali region.

RELIGIONS

There are three main religions in Nigeria. Islam and Christianity are both popular, and many people also remain faithful to parts of the ancient tribal beliefs.

NIGERIA has more people than any other country in Africa. Almost half of the country's population are Muslims. They follow the Islamic faith. About a third of the people are Christians. Some are Catholics and others are Protestants. Only one in five Nigerians still follows the traditional beliefs, but Protestant churches often mix these old beliefs with Christianity.

ISLAM is the name of the faith followed by Muslims. They believe in one supreme god called Allah. Islam was started in the 7th century by the prophet Mohammed.

This elaborate metal cross shows how Nigerians have adapted traditional art to the symbols of Christianity.

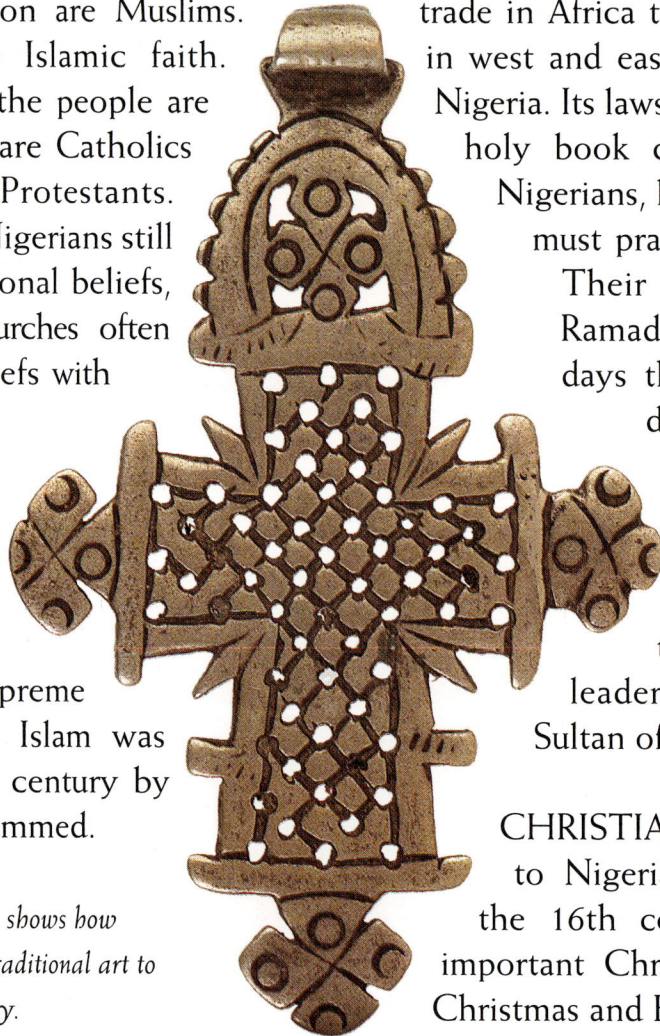

It began in Arabia and soon spread to north Africa. Through the Arab slave trade in Africa the faith took hold in west and east Africa, including Nigeria. Its laws are contained in a holy book called the Koran. Nigerians, like other Muslims, must pray five times a day. Their main festival is Ramadan, when for 30 days they cannot eat or drink during the hours of daylight. Nigerian Muslims live mainly in the north of the country. Their leader is called the Sultan of Sokoto.

CHRISTIANITY first came to Nigeria from Europe in the 16th century. The most important Christian festivals are Christmas and Easter.

ANIMISM is the name given to old tribal beliefs. It means that things such as rivers and trees can possess spirits. These spirits are worshipped with dance, prayers and sacrifice. Traditionally, people worshipped the dead, who were thought to be very wise. People used masks to summon up the spirits in their rituals.

FOLK SONGS

There are no Nigerian folk songs in this book. Nigerian folk songs are not written down like other songs. Instead the tunes and words vary according to the occasion. They are different every time. Because there are no songs in this book does not mean that music is not important. All over Nigeria you can hear drums, singing and traditional instruments.

GREETINGS FROM **NIGERIA!**

Nigeria's population of some 95 million people belongs to more than 250 different groups. The biggest are the Hausa people of the north, the Yoruba of the southwest and the Ibo of the southeast. Together they make up over half the population.

English is the official language, which comes from the days when Britain ruled Nigeria. But most people also speak Hausa, Yoruba or Ibo, depending on where they live. The greetings translated here are in Yoruba. In southern Nigeria many people speak pidgin English. This began as a kind of simple English, but has now developed into a complex language of its own.

How do you say...

Hello
She alaafia ni

Goodbye
O daabo

Thank you
E shee

Peace
Ohilaja

7

LEBOKU

The Yakurr people of southern Nigeria celebrate the harvest with a whole week of traditional rituals and dancing.

In August each year the Yakurr people celebrate *Leboku*, the festival that marks the yam harvest. Yams are roots, a little like sweet potatoes. They are the Yakurr's main crop, so a good harvest is a reason to celebrate.

Leboku lasts seven days. The Yakurr hold feasts and rituals. But the real heart of the celebration is dancing to furious drumming. It is a noisy affair. The drummers begin playing as early as 4 a.m.

There are two main dances. *Ekoi* is for men, and *Ekeledei* is for women. The Ekoi is the Yakurr's chief. Drummers use "talking" drums, which sound like an African language, to call the Ekoi and the high priests to the

dance. They all wear costumes, and their feet are painted. They wave small brushes. Two men dance the Ekoi. They have sheep fleece on their arms and wave swords. The dance is based on ancient movements for fighting.

Ekeledei girls wear brass leg rings up to their knees and cloth ankle bands. They adorn their hair with fine peacock feathers. They decide the order to stand in during the dance by holding a wrestling tournament.

Another big part of Leboku is called *Yekpi*, which is similar to April Fool's Day.

This instrument is made from a hollow gourd and is decorated with elaborate carving. Small brushes of horse hair like this one are waved during the dance to brush away evil spirits. They also keep away the flies.

Young men perform feats of strength that they say are done by magic. People pretend to be rude to each other. On this day everybody has fun.

Women wear decorated beads like this to protect their ankles from their brass leg rings as they dance the Ekeledei.

YAM FUFU

SERVES 4–6
900g yams
Salt (optional)
Banana leaves, to serve (optional)

1 Using a vegetable peeler, peel the yams. Cut into chunks.
2 Bring a large pan of water to the boil over a high heat. Add the yam chunks and return the water to the boil. Boil until the yam chunks are very tender.
3 Drain the yams in a colander in the sink.
4 Using a pestle and mortar, or a potato masher, mash the yams until smooth, like mashed potatoes. Add salt if you like.
5 Spoon on to banana leaves or into a bowl to serve. This is traditionally served with stews.

9

THE MAGIC DRUM

It is hard work tilling the land to grow food to feed your family.

Often the weather turns bad and the crops fail. This is a story

about the great importance of work and the harvest.

ONCE UPON A TIME there lived a very wise king. Nobody in his kingdom ever went hungry, even when the harvest failed. The king had a magic drum, and whenever the harvest was poor, he drummed on it. Vast amounts of food would appear, spread out on tables ready to eat. Then the king held huge feasts, to which he invited everyone who lived nearby, and even some of the local animals. The only thing that the king was not generous with was his drum. He guarded it carefully, as it was the source of food for his people.

Tortoise, the laziest animal in the forest, was plotting to take the drum away and keep the food for himself and his own family. He did not think of other people's hunger in time of famine.

One day the queen and her daughter were taking a walk when a coconut fell and broke open in front of them. High up on a rock, Tortoise waited. "What good luck," thought the queen and gave it to her daughter to eat. As soon as the little girl had finished the fruit, Tortoise rolled down from the high rock where he was spying.

He shouted, "Give me back my coconut." The queen simply smiled.

When they all got back to the village Tortoise told the king that he, Tortoise, had worked very hard for the coconut that had been taken from him.

"I will repay you," said the king. "You can have anything that you want."

Immediately Tortoise replied, "I'll have your magic drum." The queen was

amazed when the king agreed and gave it to Tortoise. The king did not tell Tortoise that if its owner were ever to walk over a stick in his path, the drum refused to make food. Instead, when it was used, three hundred angry warriors would appear, and beat the drummer. The king knew that Tortoise was bound to step over a stick as he plodded along.

Sure enough, Tortoise came back the next day, covered in dents. "I have come to return your drum," he said. "Instead of a feast I got a beating." "Thank you, Tortoise," said the king, "this drum is like the land, in the right hands it yields a good harvest. If you are mean and lazy, you and your family will always go hungry."

FISHING FESTIVAL

For more than 400 years the end of the fishing season has been marked by a festival at Argungu, on the River Rima in the northwest of Nigeria.

The date of the festival changes from year to year. It usually takes place on a Saturday in February or early in March. The precise day is set by the Emir of Argungu, the local ruler. He is also the guest of honour at the festival.

Nigeria has a great many rivers, and fish are therefore a very important food. This famous fishing festival began in the 16th century, to mark the end of the fishing season.

The festival takes place at a pavilion built beside the river. The events include archery, wrestling and boxing, as well as music and dancing.

The main event is a fishing competition. Hundreds of men form a line over a kilometre long a short

This statuette shows the Emir of Argungu being protected from the sun by a parasol. The decorated fabric is designed to celebrate the festival.

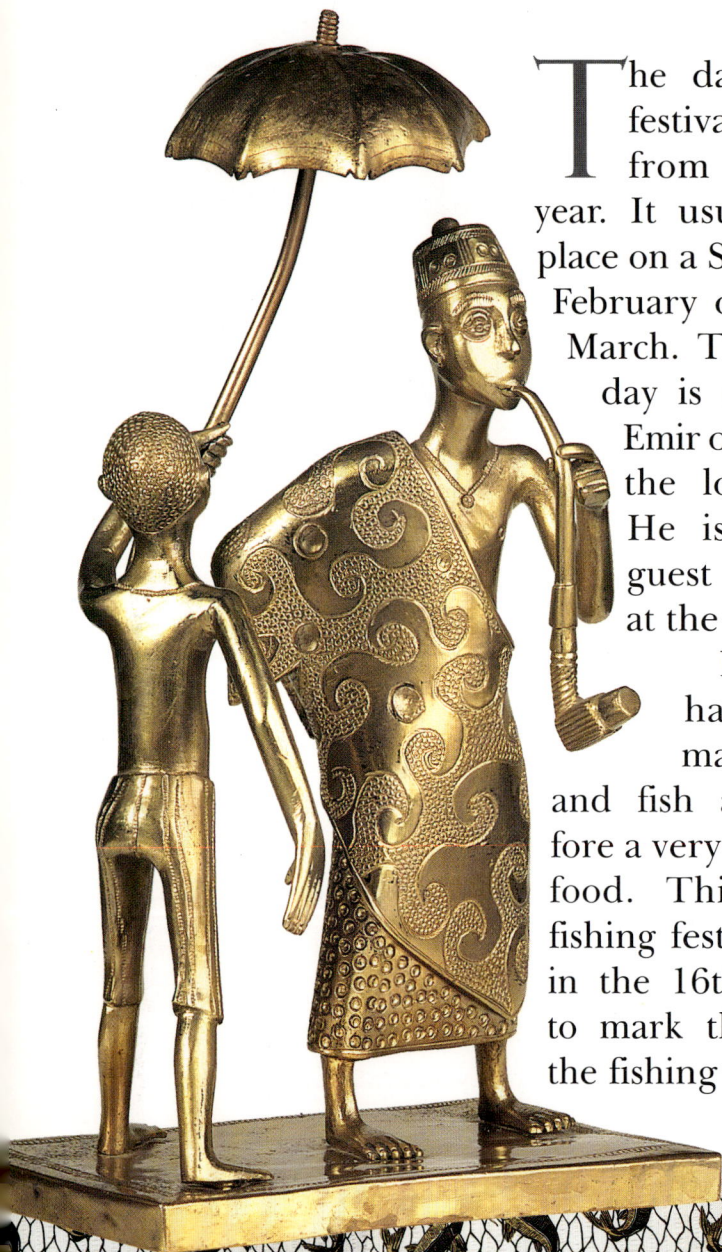

distance from the river. Each carries a large hollow gourd and two nets, which look like the wings of a huge butterfly. This is the traditional way of fishing in Nigeria.

With a sign from the Emir a gun is fired. The fishermen charge forward into the river, which becomes a seething mass of men and nets. After two hours another shot signals the end of the competition. Whoever catches the largest fish gets a prize. The season is over on the river for another year.

Nigerians preserve fish by drying them in salt. Before refrigeration this was the main way of preserving fish all over the world. The fish tastes strong and salty.

FISH STEW

SERVES 6

15g fresh parsley, finely chopped
1 onion, finely chopped
½ red pepper, finely chopped
1kg fish fillets, skinned
75ml peanut oil
3 tbsp tomato purée
125ml fish stock or water
75g each sliced red and green peppers
200g potatoes, diced

1 Combine parsley, onions, and chopped pepper in a bowl.
2 Place some of the parsley mixture on top of one fillet. Roll over. Secure with a tooth pick. Repeat with remaining fillets.
3 Heat the oil in a flameproof casserole. Add the fish and fry until brown. Stir in tomato purée, stock and diced potatoes. Add any left-over parsley mixture and sliced peppers. Cover.
4 Simmer 20 minutes, until potatoes are cooked.

MMANWE FESTIVAL

This annual festival celebrates tribal tradition. Craftsmen display their masks and perform to the beat of "talking" drums.

Masks no longer play as significant a role in Nigerian life as they once did. But they still feature in spectacular ceremonies held each December in the south of the country, where a very important festival is held in the province of Anambra.

Many masks are based on the animals of the bush. Tribal people usually live quite near wild creatures and they naturally borrow designs from, say, the spots of a leopard or a zebra's stripes.

Among these people there are

By holding the strings of this drum, drummers make it sound as if it is talking the Yoruba language.

secret societies that choose certain animals as their "totems" or emblems. They hope that if they resemble that animal, they will become as fierce or brave as it is.

Nigerians used to believe that masks

Elaborate masks help the people who wear them take on a different character, which might be that of an ancestor or of a particular animal, such as a giraffe.

Today's festivals are held to preserve the old mask-making traditions, despite the fact that the beliefs behind the masks are no longer remembered or are not important.

A festival high-light is the display of rare masks. The most powerful of all is known as *Ijele*, which means king of masks.

allowed people to take on the character of their ancestors, whom they used to worship. By wearing masks, people thought that they could be as wise as their respected ancestors.

MAKE YOUR OWN MASK

African masks were carved and decorated with bones, claws and teeth. Make your own, but pattern it with raffia, buttons and feathers.

The masks of Africa used to play an important role in tribal life. The magic men of medicine wore them; the priests and judges hid behind them. Masks covered the ordinary human face and brought special qualities to the wearer. The people who were not in masks felt the power of the mask and would do whatever the masked one told them to do. Masks often resembled animals. Certain qualities of the animal were exaggerated. A leopard-mask may be given a huge row of sharp teeth, or the pale, sharp eyes of a lion would become big and scary on the mask. Masks were made to frighten. The masked one could pick out a wrongdoer or a criminal. The mask would scare the guilty person into a confession.

Masks are now works of art, showing the skill of the craftsman. Make one to put on the wall or wear to a party.

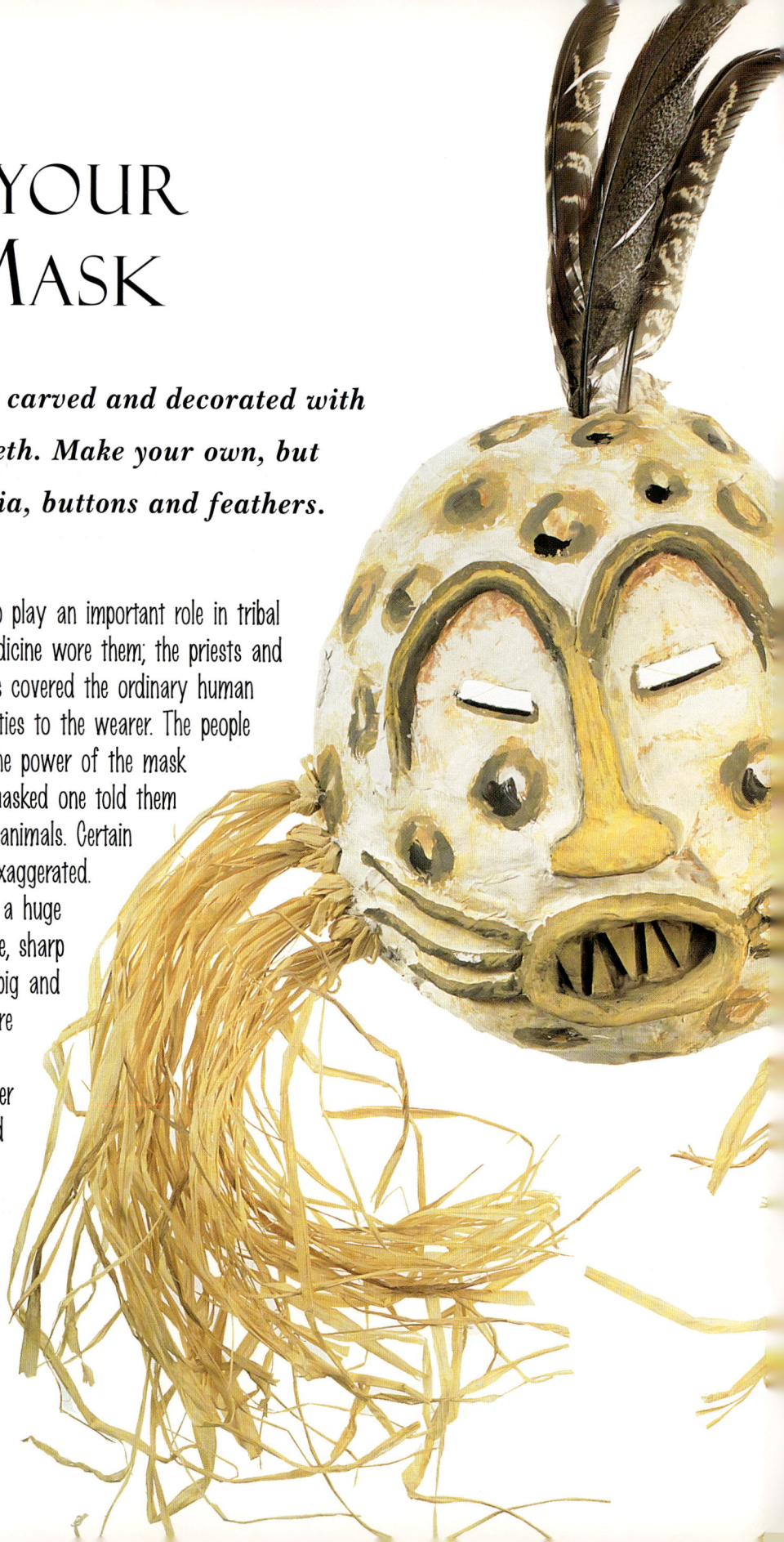

YOU WILL NEED
A balloon
Newspaper and cardboard
Wallpaper paste
Poster paints
Raffia
Feathers

1 Blow up a balloon to the size and shape of your head. Cover the balloon with long strips of newspaper, painted with wallpaper paste. Tie a string to the knot of the balloon and hang it up to dry. Draw a clear line around the papier-mâché sphere, and then cut it in half with a pair of scissors. Discard one of the halves, or use it make a second mask. You now have your basic mask shape.

2 Cover the cut edges of the half-sphere with small scraps of newspaper and wallpaper paste. Make the eyebrows, nose, mouth and whiskers with pieces of twisted newspaper that have been covered with paste. Allow them to dry, then stick on the cardboard teeth. Paint the mask white, then leave it to dry once more.

3 Decorate the mask with poster paints. Once the paint has dried, poke a hole in the centre of each eye, to see through. Then poke four holes along the edge of the mask near the whiskers. Thread the strips of raffia through these holes. Finally stick some feathers to the top of the mask.

REGATTA

Every year Nigerians celebrate the role rivers play in their lives with festivals that end in spectacular canoe races.

Nigerians have always maintained close links with the many rivers, large and small, that flow through their country. These rivers provide the people with a good supply of fish.

They also irrigate the land for growing crops. In some parts of the country the rivers are still the easiest way to travel. People use canoes to make trips or even to go to school or to buy food.

The rivers are so important that some people think of them as gods and goddesses.

Regattas, or boat races, began as a way of giving thanks to these deities. Most riverside settlements hold regattas, but the

A model canoe shows people taking food to the market. Musicians play traditional instruments like the calabash (top) at regattas.

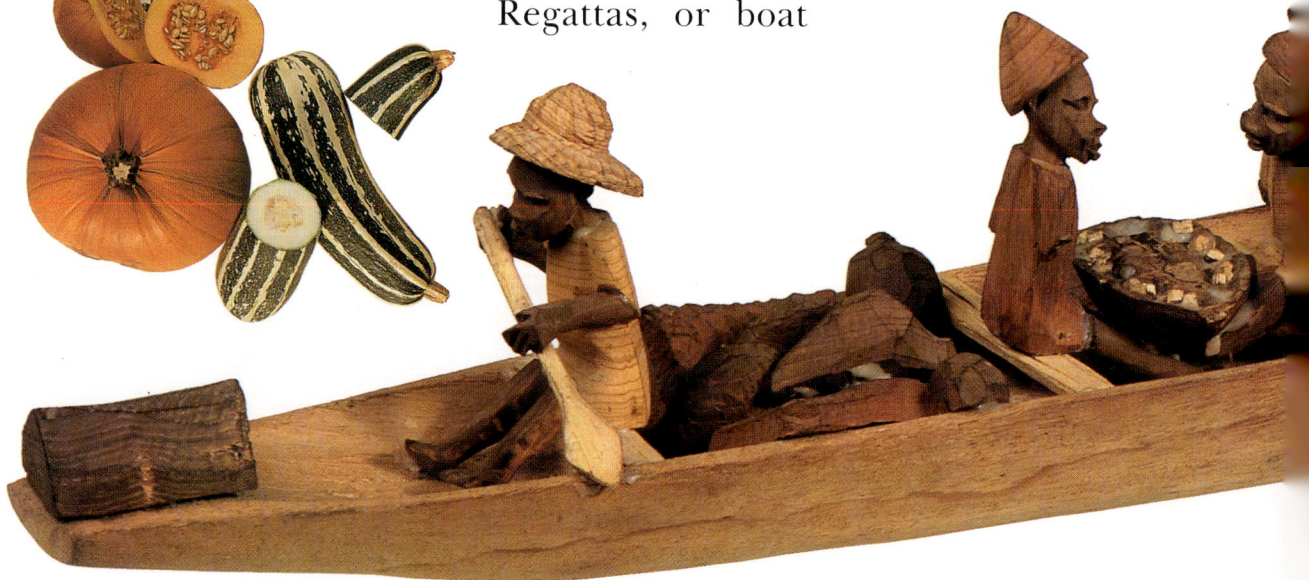

most famous one is at Pategi, on the Niger.

The regatta is held near the river. There are dances representing many kinds of water creature, and everyone takes a picnic and watches displays by swimmers and acrobats.

The highlight is a rowing race in brightly painted canoes. Strong rowers paddle the boats. Winning is not as important as taking part in an event that is enjoyed by everyone.

The most common form of jewellery in Nigeria is long strings of beads that people wear for special occasions like the regatta. As they have been for hundreds of years, the beads are made of polished glass and brightly coloured stones.

OSUN CEREMONY

Every year the Yoruba people of southwest Nigeria worship the goddess of their local river with rituals, music and sacrifices.

The old legends tell the story that the rivers were not always there. The rivers were once women. They were changed into rivers by the gods. The River Osun was a goddess. On the last Friday of August the Yoruba people worship her. The rituals take place around three shrines in Oshogbo, a town in the Yoruba country.

Rituals are led by the Ataoja, the ruler of Oshogbo. The Atacja offers sacrifices to other gods of the area to ask them to help win the blessings of Osun. Drummers and singers follow him as he parades through the town's streets.

The king also gives gifts to his people. He holds a feast for the rich people and gives presents to all his poor subjects. These celebrations last for seven days. They go on throughout the night. On the eighth day the main ritual takes place on the

Kola nuts are offered to the river goddess. They are an important crop for the local people. The bronze warrior is from Benin, the Yorubas' old kingdom. Similar figures are placed near shrines.

Chickens are among the sacrifices made to Osun. Worshippers believe that the goddess likes good things to eat. The more valuable the animal, the more pleased she will be to receive it.

banks of the river. A young priestess, called the Arugba, is led forwards. She is painted all over, and must hold two kola nuts, uneaten, in her mouth for the whole day. In a trance, she leads a procession to the river, where the Ataoja feeds the river fish to please the Osun.

The women crowd around the river. They ring bells, pray to the goddess and drink river water. The Osun festival ends in great rejoicing.

THE RIVER GODDESS

There are many stories about Osun, the river goddess.

They are also found in Brazil, taken there by Yorubas.

The stories explain our need for rain and rivers, and

how all life depends on a supply of water.

THIS IS THE STORY of Laro, a king who lived many years ago. He ruled over Osogbo, a village surrounded by farms and country folk, and built near the banks of the mighty River Osun.

Everyone in Osogbo depended on this river. They drove their animals down to the river to drink, and during the dry season they carried its water back to their parched fields. They built boats to row swiftly and to go fishing.

One year the rains did not come when they were supposed to. There was no rain for months. There was no longer a river, but a muddy stream. The crops dried up in the fields, and the farm animals and the wild ones started dying.

People were hungry and frightened.

King Laro consulted the elders. The old men reminded him that the Osun was more than a river. Long ago the river had been a human woman, but she had turned into water and become a goddess. Osun was clearly upset with King Laro and his people. But the king did not know why, and neither did his people. The animals gazed at him.

Very early one morning Laro climbed down to the empty riverbed and called out, "Osun, why are you punishing my people and all the animals?"

The king waited and waited until he was hot and very thirsty. He bowed his head on the dry riverbed. Suddenly

King Laro heard a soft voice, a voice like the tiny waves of the mighty Osun.

"You and your village have only ever taken from me," said the voice. "You never give anything back. You must sacrifice the farm animals to me. Give my fish your last supplies of yam and plantain and fufu flour."

"We have almost nothing left," the king whispered sadly. "We will die."

"You must give me everything you have," replied the wavelike voice, "and I will take care of you and the beasts."

Laro nodded his head in obedience. He waited for more, but there were no voices, no sounds, only the sun and the silent animals lying in the shade.

The next day King Laro sacrificed the last three animals in the village – a goat and two chickens. He lifted the gourds and shook the last of the grain onto the dry riverbed. As he finished, the sky turned dark with a huge rain cloud. Water fell from the sky.

Although the rain did not stop for three days, the animals galloped with joy; the people leapt into their boats and fished in the river. They ran to their fields to start planting. Osun kept her promise. She would look after them if they cared for her. And every year since, on the same day the people of Osogbo have brought their sacrifices and grain to the river.

SALLAH

The Islamic fast called Ramadan takes place at different times each year. Nigeria's Muslims celebrate the end of the 30-day fast with Sallah.

This stringed instrument is a little like a guitar, with a hollow box that amplifies the vibrations made by the five strings.

Muslims are supposed to fast in *Ramadan*, the ninth month of the Muslim year. They are not allowed to eat or drink between sunrise and sunset. At the end of the long fast everyone has a grand celebration.

The main Sallah celebrations take place in northern Nigeria, where most Muslims live. The most elaborate festival is in the town of Katsina. Here, thousands gather for the main event. This is the *Durbar,* a colourful procession of horsemen in bright, ornate costumes. Durbar is an old Persian word that means house or court.

The first Durbars were held when the British used to rule Nigeria. The British ruler, who was called the *viceroy,* held magnificent ceremonies to show the Nigerians that the British were in charge. After the British left Nigeria, the Nigerians still held the Durbar. There are

Muslim ruler, called the *Emir*. He rides in the middle of the parade. Before him come horsemen of the Hausa-Fulani people. They wear coats of armour, scarlet turbans and copper helmets topped with plumes of feathers. The horses have decorated manes and tails, and brightly coloured bridles.

Then comes the Emir, in robes of white and carrying a parasol embroidered with silver. After the Emir are his guards, then wrestlers flexing their muscles. The crowd dances and sings to the musicians playing their drums, lutes and fiddles.

For the Sallah, everyone puts on clothes made of bright cloth like this. The warriors carry heavily decorated weapons.

people who think that it belongs to the past and has no place in Nigeria now that it is independent.

The focus of the Durbar is the local

HOW TO MAKE A FAN

These fans are identical copies of Nigerian designs, but ours are made from materials to be found at home and not of leather and ostrich feathers.

In northern Nigeria the climate is hot, the land dusty, and often it is windless. Fans are useful. They make little waves of cool air and keep away insects. The craftsmen of Nigeria are not content to make simply useful fans but create bold, beautiful ones. These fans are not pleated and folded, as are European and Oriental fans. The Nigerians make solid semicircles or large curved shapes from hardened leather. They decorate these with wool or paint, and stick shells or buttons on them. Feathers are added for extra grandeur.

On this page we have decorated one fan with a raffia fringe, while the other has feathers around the edge. African artwork tends to be geometric. This means that angular shapes are used, and the artists prefer bright colours that are not overwhelmed in the bright sunshine. Choose colours that bring an "authentic" Nigerian touch to the fan you make.

At a Durbar fans can be seen all over the place, but the chiefs amd Emirs have the grandest and most decorative. This is partly because the craftsmen want to please them, but it is also a sign of their status as leaders.

In Nigeria the fringe of this fan might be made of ostrich or eagle feathers. We used raffia.

1 Take a piece of cardboard about 60cm long and 20cm wide. Fold it in half. Cut the open corners, two at a time, so that they curve to form an arch shape. Cover one of the surfaces with paint and wait for it to dry. This will be the front of your fan. Now unfold the cardboard and cut a 5cm-wide slit in the centre of the fold.

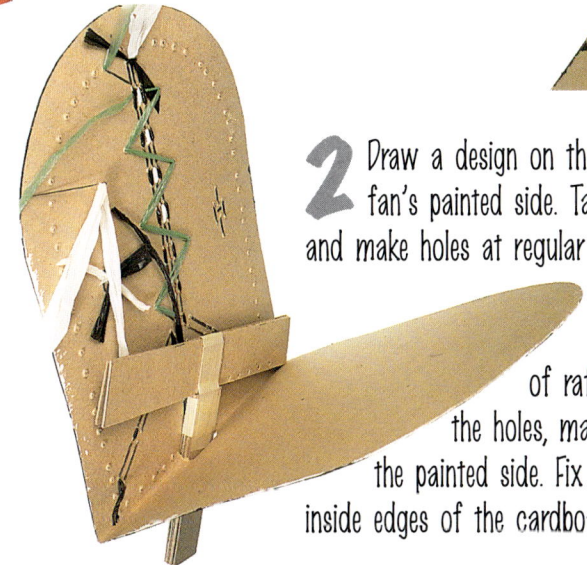

2 Draw a design on the reverse of the fan's painted side. Take a craft needle, and make holes at regular intervals along the lines of your design. Thread the lengths of raffia or wool through the holes, making a pattern on the painted side. Fix the feathers to the inside edges of the cardboard with sticky tape.

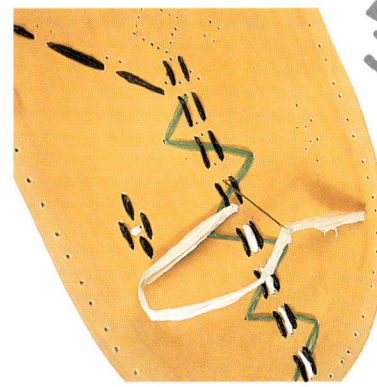

3 Cut out two pieces of cardboard, each about 15cm long and 5cm wide, and tape them together into a T-shape. Slide the trunk of the "T" through the slit to make a handle. Wrap raffia or wool around it until it feels comfortable to hold. Stick the two sides of the fan together with glue. Finally, stitch the top of the "T" to the fan with raffia or wool.

YOU WILL NEED

Sheets of cardboard or a cardboard box
Strips of raffia or wool
Feathers
A craft needle, some glue and sticky tape
Poster paints

CHRISTMAS

Christmas is the most important festival of the year for more than 30 million Nigerian Christians.

Christmas in Nigeria is very like Christmas festivities held elsewhere. In the 19th century many Christian missionaries came to Nigeria from Europe. They brought their European Christmas traditions with them. Santa Claus comes on Christmas Eve and presents are opened on Christmas morning, just as they are in many parts of Europe and America.

A few Christmas traditions in Nigeria

Palm branches hung with Christmas balls decorate the homes of most Nigerians. Only the rich can afford pine or plastic trees.

are different, however. There are no pine trees in Nigeria, so most families decorate a palm tree instead. Wealthy people buy pine trees imported from Europe.

Chicken is usually the Christmas meal. Meat is expensive in Nigeria, so for many it is a great festive treat.

JOLLOFF CHICKEN

SERVES 4–6

3 tomatoes
3 onions
Vegetable oil for frying
450g chicken pieces,
skin removed
3 red peppers, cored, seeded
and chopped
300g long grain rice
Chicken stock
Salt and pepper

1 Slice 1 tomato and chop 2. Slice 1 onion and chop 2.

2 Heat 2 tbsp oil in frying pan. Fry onion slices for 5 minutes. Add the tomato slices and fry 1 minute longer; set aside.

3 Add 2 tbsp oil to the pan. Fry the chicken on both sides. Remove from pan.

4 Put chopped tomatoes, onions and peppers in pan. Fry until soft. Stir in rice. Put chicken on top. Add enough chicken stock to cover.

5 Bring to the boil. Cover and simmer 30 minutes. Stir in the onion and tomato slices and heat through. Add salt and pepper.

This nativity scene combines the familiar figures and animals with simple Nigerian carving and colours.

29

INDEPENDENCE DAY

For centuries Nigeria fell to different rulers. The Benin empire rose and faded; sultans held sway. The British took power. But now Nigerians control their own country.

Nigeria became independent from British rule on October 1, 1960. The country had been a British colony for 60 years. It was one of the first African colonies in the British Empire to gain self-rule. Each year the Nigerians remember the proud day when they took charge of their own country.

The early years of independence were not easy in Nigeria. Civil war split the land as rival groups fought and tried to get power. A million Nigerians died.

Today October 1 is a day for everybody to celebrate what they have in common with each other, rather than the differences they feel between them.

Independence Day is a holiday for all the people. Some will go to grand balls, some to street parties or family dinners, as all Nigerians rejoice in the achievements of their nation.

On Independence Day the streets are full of people. Many are dressed in beautifully embroidered clothes or fabrics, carrying symbols of their country and images of heroes and leaders.

WORDS TO KNOW

Animism: The belief that things in nature, such as rivers and trees, possess spirits and, sometimes, supernatural powers.

Calabash: A hollow gourd used as a container or made into a musical instrument.

Deity: A god or goddess.

Emblem: A picture that represents an idea.

Emir: The title given to a Muslim ruler. A Nigerian tribal chieftain.

Fast: To go without food deliberately.

Fufu flour: A basic food in African diets. It is made from ground roots (such as yams) and grains.

Gourd: A large tropical fruit, similar to a pumpkin, that has a very hard skin.

Irrigate: To supply the land, especially the crops, with water artificially.

Pavilion: A decorative building that is used for entertainment or sports.

Pidgin: A simplified language that contains words from two or more languages. A pidgin language helps people who do not share a common language to communicate. In time, a pidgin can become a complicated language on its own.

Plantain: Banana-like fruit that is eaten cooked.

Regatta: A sports event featuring boat races.

Ritual: A religious ceremony that must be performed in a certain way or order.

Sallah: In Nigeria the celebration that marks the end of the Islamic fast period of Ramadan.

Totem: An admired animal or natural object that a tribal person or group chooses as its emblem.

Trance: A mysterious, sleep-like state that is difficult to wake from.

ACKNOWLEDGMENTS

WITH THANKS TO:

Africa Centre, London fly whisk p8, drum, dolls p14, wooden animals, musical instruments p20-24. Anthony Adeloye p30. Nigerian High Commission, London mask, cross p6-7, gourd p8, mask p14, brass figure p21. Vale Antiques, Elgin Avenue, London brass figure p12.

PHOTOGRAPHS BY:

All photographs by Bruce Mackie. Cover photograph by ZEFA.

ILLUSTRATIONS BY:

Alison Fleming title page, Robert Shadbolt p4-5, Mountain High Maps ® Copyright © 1993 Digital Wisdom, Inc. p4-5. Philip Divine p7. Philip Bannister p11. Norman Bancroft-Hunt p22-23.

INDEX

Contents

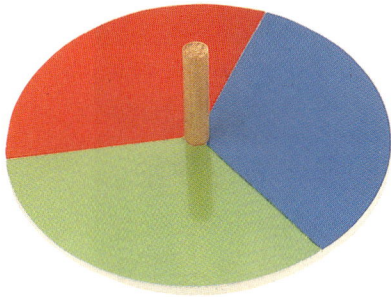

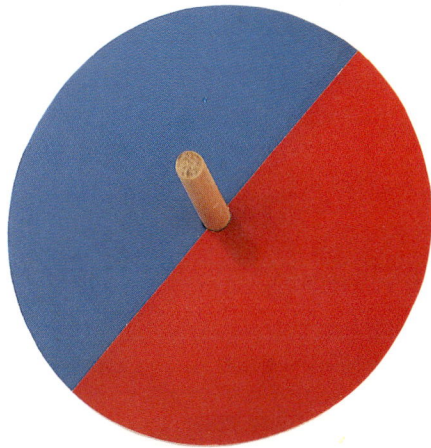

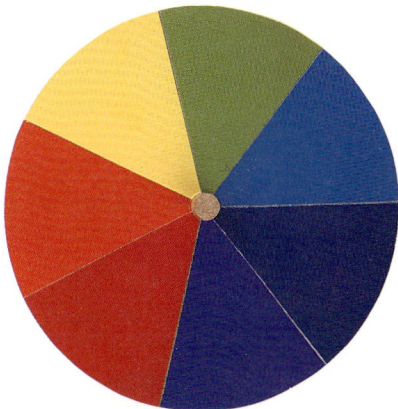

Introduction

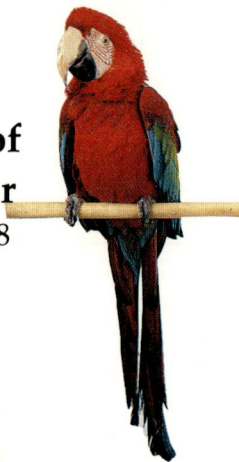

Look around you, then shut your eyes. You have closed off much of the world that is familiar. You soon realise that you need **light** for so many things in everyday life.

We need light for nearly everything we do. We use it to find our way, to show us a programme on the TV, to signal the traffic, even to send messages by telephone.

Light even brings the **energy** that plants use to grow. Without light we would simply have no food to eat.

Colour is also very important to us. We use colour when we choose our clothes, we use colour to control traffic,

reflections
page 14

lamps
page 8

rainbows
page 34

signals
page 10

and we rely on colours to tell us about some dangers such as fire.

Light and colour give us a great deal of pleasure. Fantastic firework displays and colourful gardens are just two of the ways that light and colour brighten our world.

In this book you will discover many exciting things about light. You will find out how light is made and how we see it. You will understand why light often plays tricks on our eyes. And you will discover some important properties of colour.

Find out about the world of light and colour in any way you choose. Just turn to a page and begin your discoveries.

lighting
page 12

shadows
page 42

shaped mirrors
page 20

Sunshine
page 6

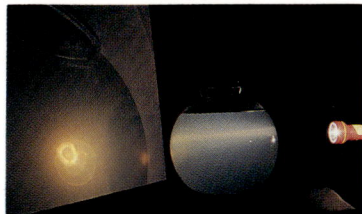

eye
page 28

telescopes
page 30

gems
page 24

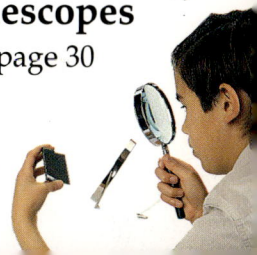

Sunlight

Natural light comes from the Sun. Even moonlight is simply light that first came from the Sun.

The Earth gets only a tiny part of the light that comes from the Sun, but it is enough to provide all the energy for our world.

Sun and sky
Our world is full of light and shadow. You can see this clearly as the light shines through a woodland in the early morning.

In this picture you can see how the light shines through as beams with straight edges. The edges to the shafts of sunlight show us that light travels in straight lines.

Sometimes the sky is covered with cloud and the Sun cannot be seen directly. The brightness in the sky then comes from the way light is scattered within the cloud.

Sky colours

We usually think of sunlight as white light, but, as we shall see later in this book, the Sun's rays can give rise to many brilliant colours. All the gold, orange and red colours of a sunset and the blue of the sky for example are produced from 'white' sunlight as it passes through the **atmosphere**.

Make a sunset

Imitate an atmosphere by filling a transparent container with water and then adding a few drops of disinfectant (the sort that makes the water go milky white). Stand the container on a sheet of white paper in bright sunlight or imitate sunlight by using a torch in a darkened room.

The more disinfectant you add the redder the light that falls on the paper will become. You have made a sunset by scattering some of the light using the disinfectant.

The sky blue can also be found. Look at the water, then at the beam of light, then along the beam of light until you see a blueish colour.

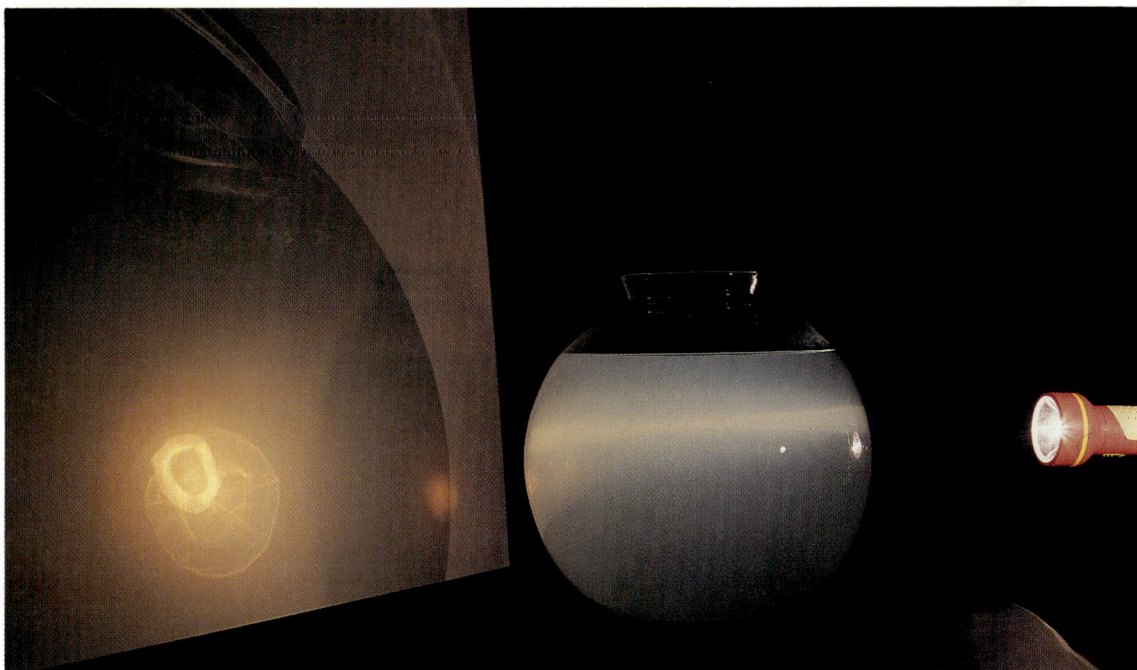

Artificial light

At night and indoors people have to make their own light. The earliest light came from camp fires and open hearths. Then came candles, oil lamps and gas lamps. Today the world mainly uses electric lamps and these come in many shapes and sizes.

Street lights, building lights and fireworks all give light to this city's night-time festival

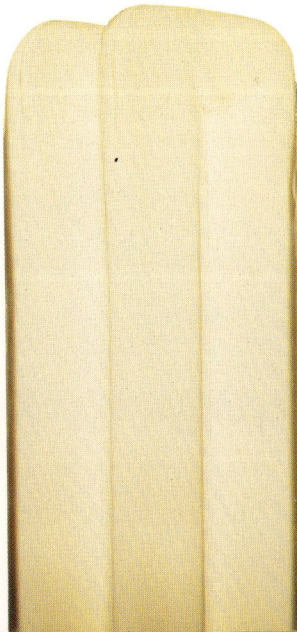

Fluorescent world

Lighting tubes give out a whiter light than bulbs. They are called **fluorescent** tubes because they are filled with a gas that shines when electricity flows through it. It then makes the special coating on the inside of the tube glow.

  Fluorescent tubes are cheaper to use than normal bulbs because they use less energy. They are most useful in shops, offices, factories and kitchens where even lighting is needed.

A compact fluorescent tube

Electric bulbs

Electric light is far brighter than candles and easier to use. With the flick of a switch you can have light where and when you want it.

The most common light comes from a light, or **incandescent**, bulb. Inside the bulb is a thin wire, called a filament, that gets hot and gives out a bright light when electricity flows through it.

Light bulbs are common in homes because they are cheap to buy and simple to fit.

In this light bulb you can see the filament glowing because it is hot

Flashing signals

People have used light as a means of signalling to each other for thousands of years. At first they used bonfires. Today we use electric light. But the purpose has stayed the same.

Lighthouses
A lighthouse is a building with a powerful signalling lantern at the top. To make the beam of light visible from many directions the beam is made to sweep across the night sky so that it appears as a series of flashes to anyone at sea. You can see the light sweeping across the sky in this picture. It is made of several narrow beams.

Each lighthouse has its own 'code signal'. Sailors simply count the time between flashes to get the code. They can then check the code on their charts and find out exactly where they are.

A light cable

Sometimes light can be trapped inside a glass rod. This is used to good effect on some toys where the light put into a bundle of rods comes out as a glittering spray at the other end.

These 'light pipes' can also be used to carry messages. Patterns of flashing light can be sent for long distances down special glass fibre cables. Telephone and computer messages are often sent this way.

Flash code

You can send signals by switching a torch on and off using a system called Morse code. This code uses patterns of short and long flashes. The Morse code for numbers is given below. The dot represents a short flash and the dash represents a long flash. Use a torch to send the time of day to your friends using the code.

• – – – – (1) •• – – –(2)••• – –(3)
•••• –(4) •••••(5) –••••6)
– –•••(7) – – –••(8) – – – –•(9)
– – – – – (10)

Bouncing light

Nearly everything in our world bounces – or reflects – light. Only truly black things reflect no light at all. We can only see things because they reflect light back to our eyes.

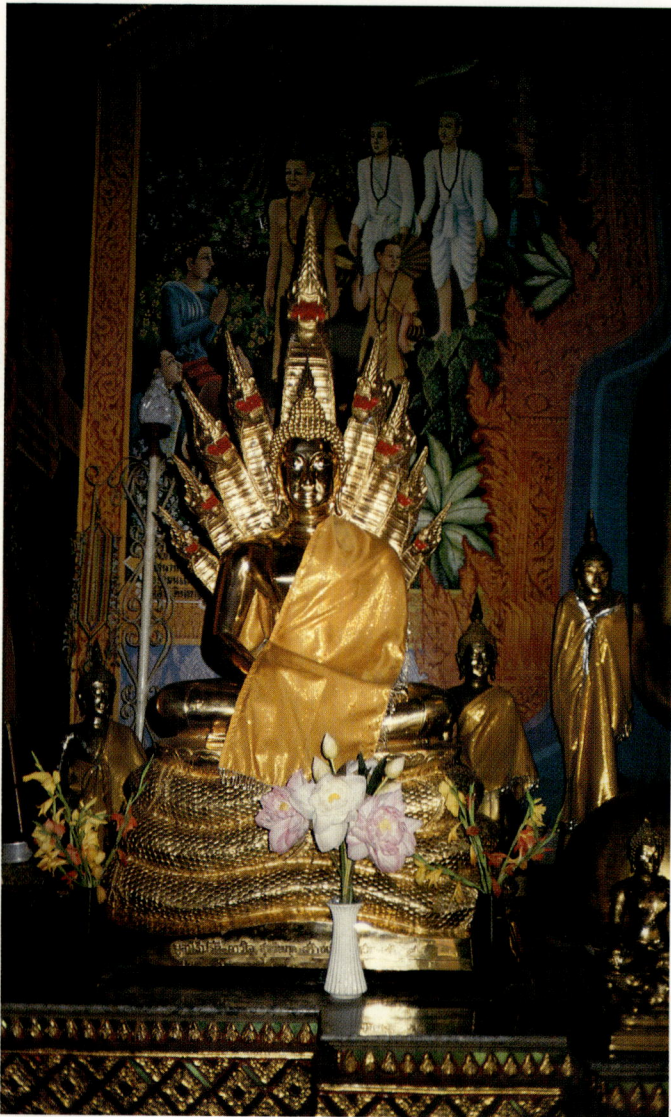

Make your own reflectors
Ask a grown-up to help you remove the shade of a table lamp. Switch the table lamp on and darken the rest of the room. The lamp will give a harsh light.

Use a piece of white paper to bounce the light. Move the paper about, watching the way the reflected light makes one part of the room brighter than another.

Ask a friend to sit beside the lamp. Use the paper to bounce light on to the shaded part of their face.

Good and bad reflectors
Reflections can be used to make things stand out or to make them less noticeable. Look at this picture of statue of the Buddha. The gold-leaf surface of the statue reflects light very well and it appears to shine. Around it there are dark materials that do not reflect the light well. Because they appear dark they do not distract our eye.

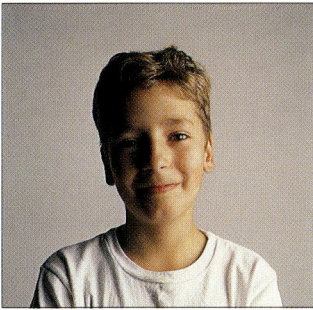

Striking effects

This picture shows you the way reflectors were used during the photography for this book. It is a 'behind the scenes' view of a studio.

The small passport-type photographs show why the circular reflector had to be used. The top picture was taken without the reflector. The lower picture was taken after the reflector had been put in place.

Notice many studio items are black so they do no give unwanted reflections. A white sheet is used to provide an even backlight.

Reflections everywhere

Light appears all around us. It is almost as though light has crept into every corner of our world. But this is only because it bounces off surfaces – reflects – so well. Even the most unlikely surfaces, such as rock, can reflect light.

Reflectors for safety
Cyclists and their bikes must be readily seen in the dark. To make them safer bikes are fitted with red or orange plastic reflectors.

Look at a bicycle reflector and investigate how it works. You should be able to count several reflecting surfaces.

Moonbounce
The world's biggest light bouncer is the Moon. You only see the Moon at night because it reflects the light from the Sun. The Moon is made of rock, but it still reflects light well. We know this because it appears so bright. The good reflection of light helps us to see details of the moon's surface.

If you were able to paint the Moon white what difference do you think it would have on our nights?

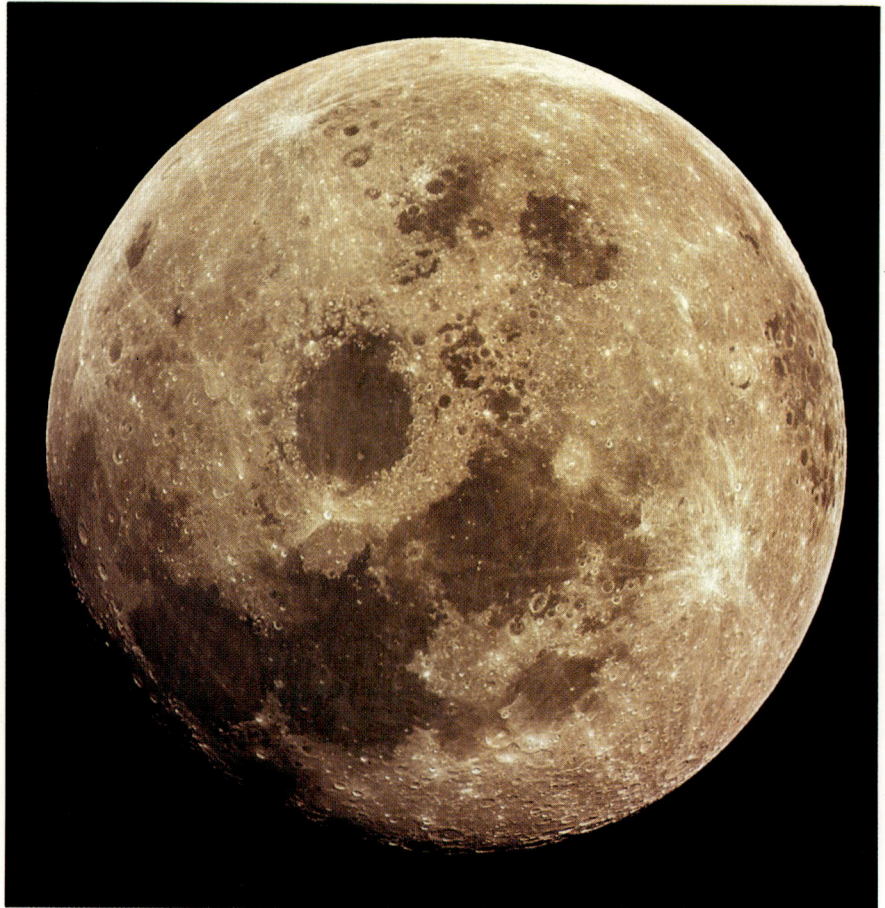

Waterbouncing

Sometimes when we look at the surface of a lake or the sea we see the water sparkling. It is reflecting the Sun's light.

Clouds, which are made from tiny water droplets, also reflect a lot of the Sun's light. The thickest clouds reflect so much light back into space that they look dark grey when seen from the ground.

Take a saucer of water and place it near a table lamp or by a sunny window. Look at it from all angles. Sometimes you can see the bottom of the saucer, but at other angles you will only see light bounced from the lamp or Sun.

Now you see it . . .
Water is **transparent**.
So when we look at this bowl from above we can clearly see the patterns painted on its surface.

. . . now you don't
When we look at the water from one side the painted inside of the bowl disappears. The reflection from a transparent material depends on the angle we look. When light is reflects clearly in this way we have made the world's most effective reflectors – a **mirror**. There is more about mirrors on the next page.

Mirror, mirror

Mirrors are the world's best reflectors. Their surfaces are so smooth that the light reflects cleanly and gives a clear picture.

Mirrors are found in many places, from the driving mirror inside a car, to huge mirrors that cover walls. Each uses reflections for a special purpose.

Did you realise you saw yourself back to front – called a mirror image?

Its all back to front
Mirrors are used inside cars to help drivers see the traffic on the road behind. But the problem is that everything is back to front. This does not matter for normal driving, but reversed writing is difficult to read.
Some emergency vehicles have reversed writing painted on to their bonnets so that other drivers driver can read the writing in their mirrors.

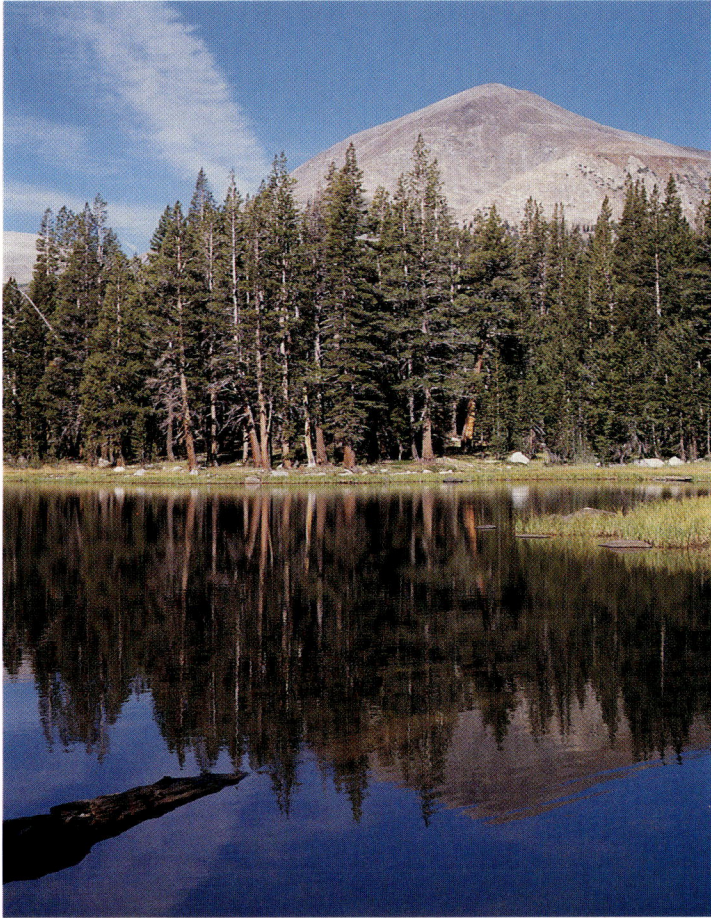

Seeing double

This mountain and forest landscape is reflected in the still waters of the lake. Notice that the reflection (called the **image**) is an exact upside down version of the real world.

The image seems to be at just the same distance as the real trees.

Place mirror against the edge of the page

Congratulations! You have now found out how to read mirror writing.

Mirror image

If you look at many insects they appear to have left and right halves that are reflections of each other.

Find out if the faces of people are also balanced. Place a mirror against this face to get a reflection and make a whole face. How does the reflected image differ from the picture on page 13? What seems wrong?

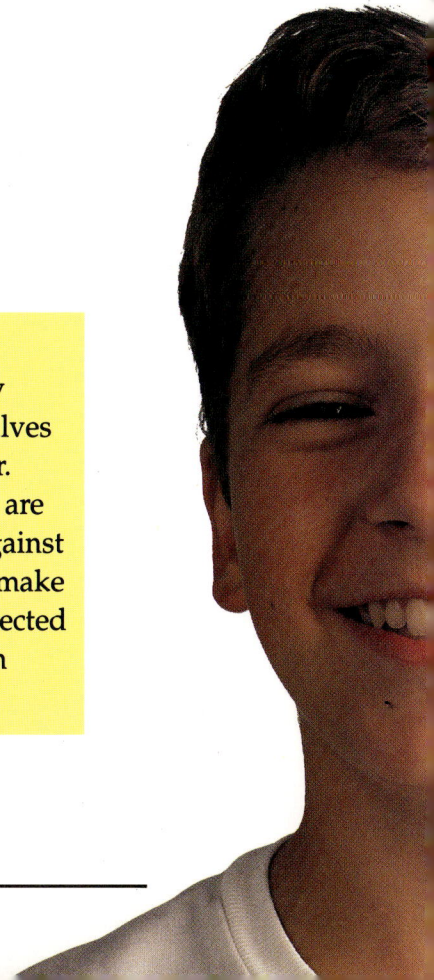

Reflecting on problems

We can use the properties of reflected light to solve all kinds of problems. On these pages you will see how mirrors are used to see round corners and to create special effects.

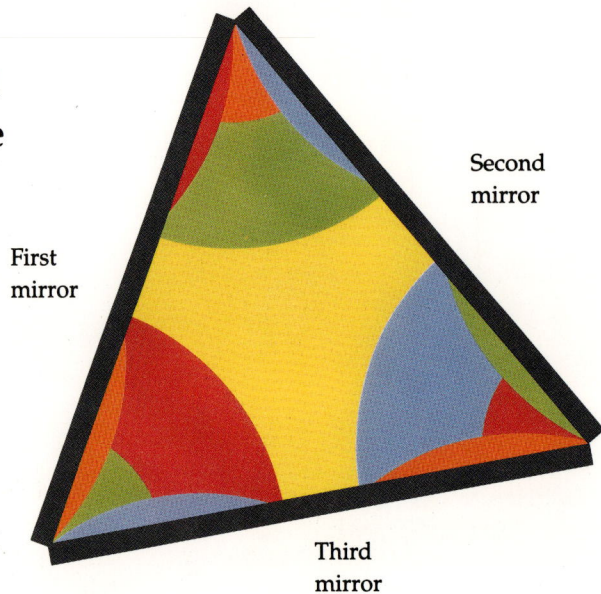

Second mirror

First mirror

Third mirror

Stand model here

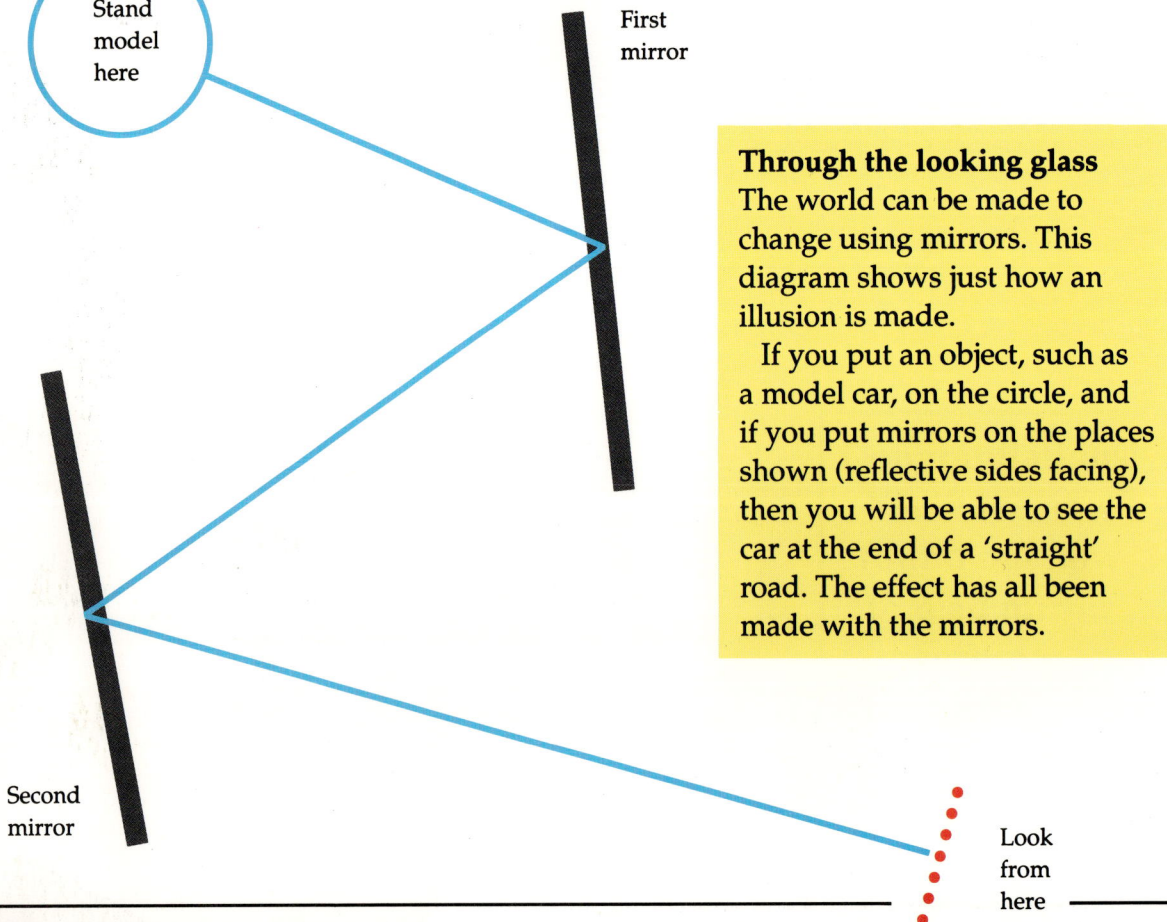

First mirror

Through the looking glass
The world can be made to change using mirrors. This diagram shows just how an illusion is made.

If you put an object, such as a model car, on the circle, and if you put mirrors on the places shown (reflective sides facing), then you will be able to see the car at the end of a 'straight' road. The effect has all been made with the mirrors.

Second mirror

Look from here

A kaleidoscope of images

You can use mirrors to make lots of strange shapes. One of the favourites is to make a **kaleidoscope**.

Put three small mirrors upright in the way shown on the left with the reflecting surfaces inside.

You can make small mirrors stand up by using sticky tape. Put small pieces of coloured paper inside the triangle of mirrors. What shapes can you see?

Put other objects inside the mirrors and look for the interesting images produced.

Tube is cut away in front of the mirror

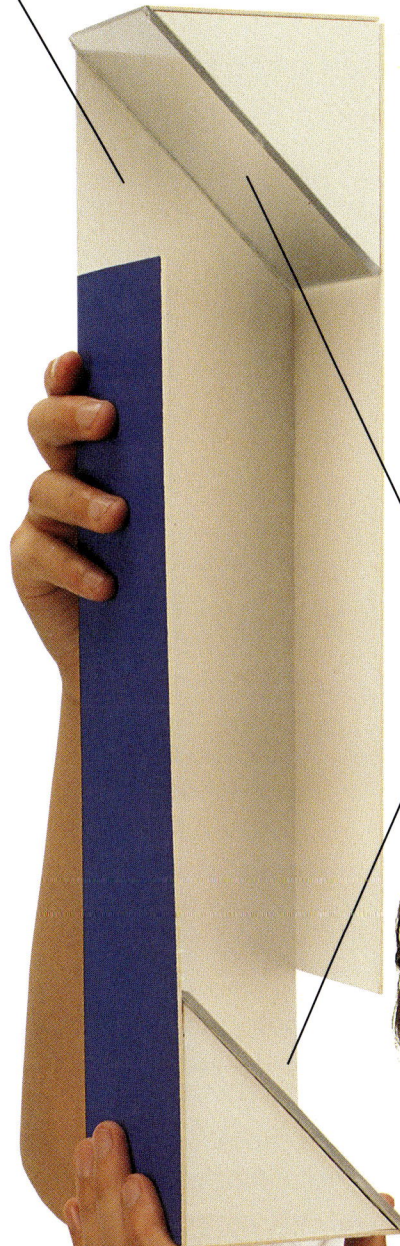

Mirrors fixed into the tube at 45 degrees

Look tall

If you have trouble seeing over the heads of a crowd then you might like to make a periscope. A periscope is an instrument for seeing objects that are not in your direct line of sight.

The periscope shown in this picture has been made from a piece of card that has been folded to make a long tube and two mirrors have been placed inside. (In the picture the side of the tube has been cut away to allow you to see the mirrors more clearly.) Ask a grown-up to help you to fix the mirrors at the correct angle.

Squashers and stretchers

There are many curved surfaces that reflect light in unusual ways. Mirrors that are shaped like the back of a spoon spread the light out over a wide area and make things look small; a dish-like mirror brings all the light together and makes things appear big. The images can look funny, but they can also be very useful.

The magic spoon
Look at yourself in a large highly polished spoon and you will see how light can be squashed and stretched.

Look at the inside of the spoon. You see yourself upside down! Move the spoon about slightly. What happens to the shape of your face?

Turn the spoon over and look at the back. Bring the spoon close to your face. What happens to your nose? What has happened to your ears? Which way up is your image.

Streetshapes
You will find many surfaces that create strangely shaped images. This picture shows the way reflections are squashed and stretched in some old panes of glass.

Getting a good view

Mirrors that curve outwards are called **convex** mirrors. They are like the back of the spoon. They give a very wide view. This is useful in car mirrors, where the driver wants to see all of the road.

Mirrors that curve inwards like the inside of a spoon are called concave mirrors. They are used in car headlights to gather the light from the lamp and turn it into a beam.

If you can get a piece of plastic mirror, you can also try the tricks shown on this page. Just bend the mirror to get the effect.

Bending light

When you look into a glass of water you may think your eyes are playing tricks. The straw in the water doesn't seem connected to the straw outside of the water. But when you remove the straw it is not bent at all.

Light changes direction whenever it passes through two different transparent substances, such as air and water or air and glass.

A mirage

A mirage is a special effect of bending light that occurs on a hot sunny day when the air near the ground gets very hot. Light rays are bent in this hot air so that you see a 'bent-round' image of the sky. The effect is to make the ground look as though it is wet even though it is perfectly dry.

In a desert people sometimes mistake a mirage for a lake of cool water even though they know the desert contains only sand and rock.

The fish that get away

In some countries it is still a tradition to go spear fishing in shallow water. But the inexperienced fishermen will often miss the fish when they throw their spears. This is because the light is bent downwards when it enters the water and so it gives a false impression of exactly where the fish is in the water.

Guess the pin

Take a **rectangular** glass or clear plastic container and put it on a piece of wood. Place two pins in the wood so that it looks like this picture. Ask someone to look through the glass along the line of the pins and then place a pin on the other side of the glass so that it appears to line up with the first two.

When they have done this stick the pin in the board, take the glass away and put a ruler against the first two pins. The chances are the third pin will be well off the line. This is because the light has been bent by the glass and the water.

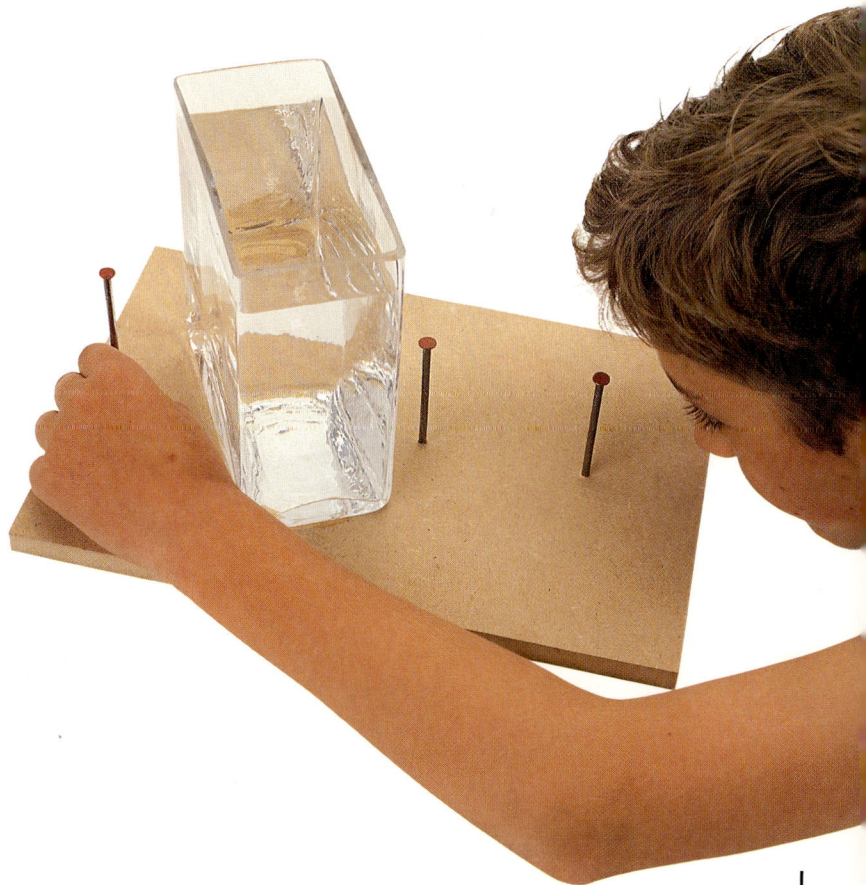

Sparkling minerals

A mineral is a natural substance found in the Earth's rocks. When a mineral forms beautifully regular shapes it is called a crystal.

Crystals can be cut to reflect and bend light in many special ways.

Crystals and gemstones

Crystals, such as the quartz crystals shown below, have a regular pattern of flat faces. Light bounces off the outside of these faces.

If the crystal is transparent, light shining from some angles may also be reflected from the inside. This inside reflection gives some crystals their sparkle when turned in the light. A cut diamond, like the one in the picture above, shows this flashing effect best.

These sparkling crystals are especially valued and are called gemstones.

Facets

Look to see the cut sides of a crystal in a piece of jewellery.

Hold the gemstone near the light, then turn it slightly. Each time the crystal flashes the light has been bounced off one of its faces or facets.

Useful sparkles help the world

A laser is a machine that turns an ordinary beam of light into a very narrow beam of extremely bright light.

At the heart of a laser there may be a crystal such as a rod of ruby (a red-coloured gemstone). When light is shone onto the crystal it is reflected many times until it becomes a very narrow bright beam.

In a supermarket lasers are used at the check-out to read the special codes on the goods. A beam of laser light is so narrow and bright it has even been bounced off the Moon and back to the Earth. The beam shown here is used by surveyors to check that the tunnel is being drilled straight.

Lenses

When you look through the flat glass of a window everything looks normal. But when you look through a curved glass, or **lens**, you find a new world.

Everything looks a different size and many things look different shapes. This is because the light rays have been bent in a very special way. Even a raindrop can be a good magnifier as this picture shows.

Lenses

A lens is a piece of transparent material with a curved surface. Most lenses have two curved surfaces facing each other.

Some lenses – those with dished or concave surfaces will make things look smaller (they are reducers); other lenses – those with bulging or convex surfaces – will make things look bigger (they are magnifiers).

A world of curved glass
Look for glass things that are curved. For example, drinking glasses (the sides and the bottoms), coffee jars, and milk bottles all made used curved glasses. To make them act as lenses, simply fill them with clean water.

Rays of light
You can find out about lenses by looking at light **rays**. You need card, a comb with large teeth and a torch. Cut a slot in a piece of cardboard and use sticky tape to fasten the teeth of a comb over the slot or simply cut teeth in the cardboard itself.

In a darkened room hold a torch to one side of the slot. The teeth turn the torch beam into separate rays.

Put each lens in front of the rays. You should see the light rays bend as in this picture.

You can group your lenses into those where the rays close up (these are the magnifiers) and those where the rays spread out (these are the reducers).

Try your ray machine with some of the other experiments in this book.

Light source

Teeth
in card
or comb

Light rays
outside lens
are straight

Drinking
glass 'lens'

Light rays are focused
to a point by the lens

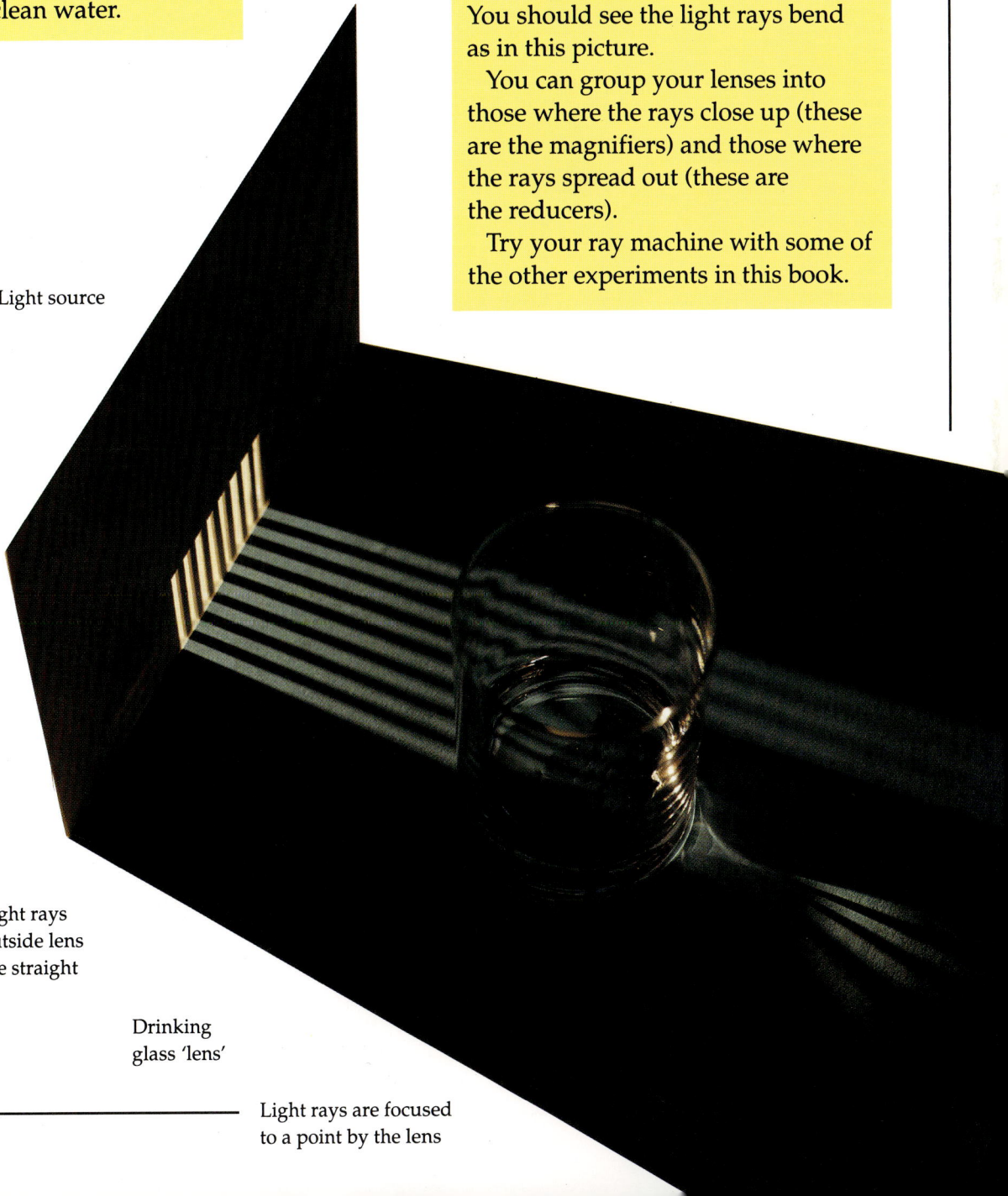

Eyes

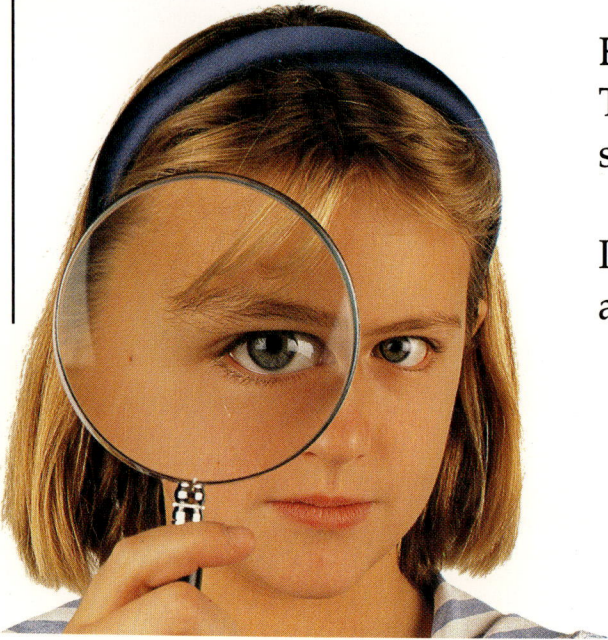

Eyes contain the world's best lenses. They also have special features for seeing clearly in bright and dim light.

The lens in an eye is a magnifier. It bulges outwards and is therefore a convex lens.

Eyes are lenses

Eyes are made with a very special soft lens that can be squashed or stretched to match the distance we want to see.

To see objects a long way off muscles in the eye change the lens into a flatter shape. To see object closely the muscles change the lens into a more round shape. All this happens without our even noticing. It is called an involuntary action.

Iris and pupil

The central coloured part of the eye is called the iris. In the centre is a hole, called the **pupil**, through which light enters the eye.

The pupil is made bigger or smaller depending on how much light is available. Also the pupil becomes slightly smaller when doing close work, such as reading. This helps to sharpen the image.

Glasses and lenses

Sometimes our eyes do not work as well as they should. Then we can help them by using add-on lenses. Some lenses can be added to the surface of the eye. They are called contact lenses. Others are placed a little way from the eyes. We call these spectacles or simply 'glasses'.

Bones of
the face

The back of the eye is called
the **retina**. This is where the
image forms. The retina is
covered with light-sensitive
cells. These give information to
the brain through **nerve** fibres

Eyebrow

Eyelid

Iris

Lens

Pupil

Muscles for
moving the eye

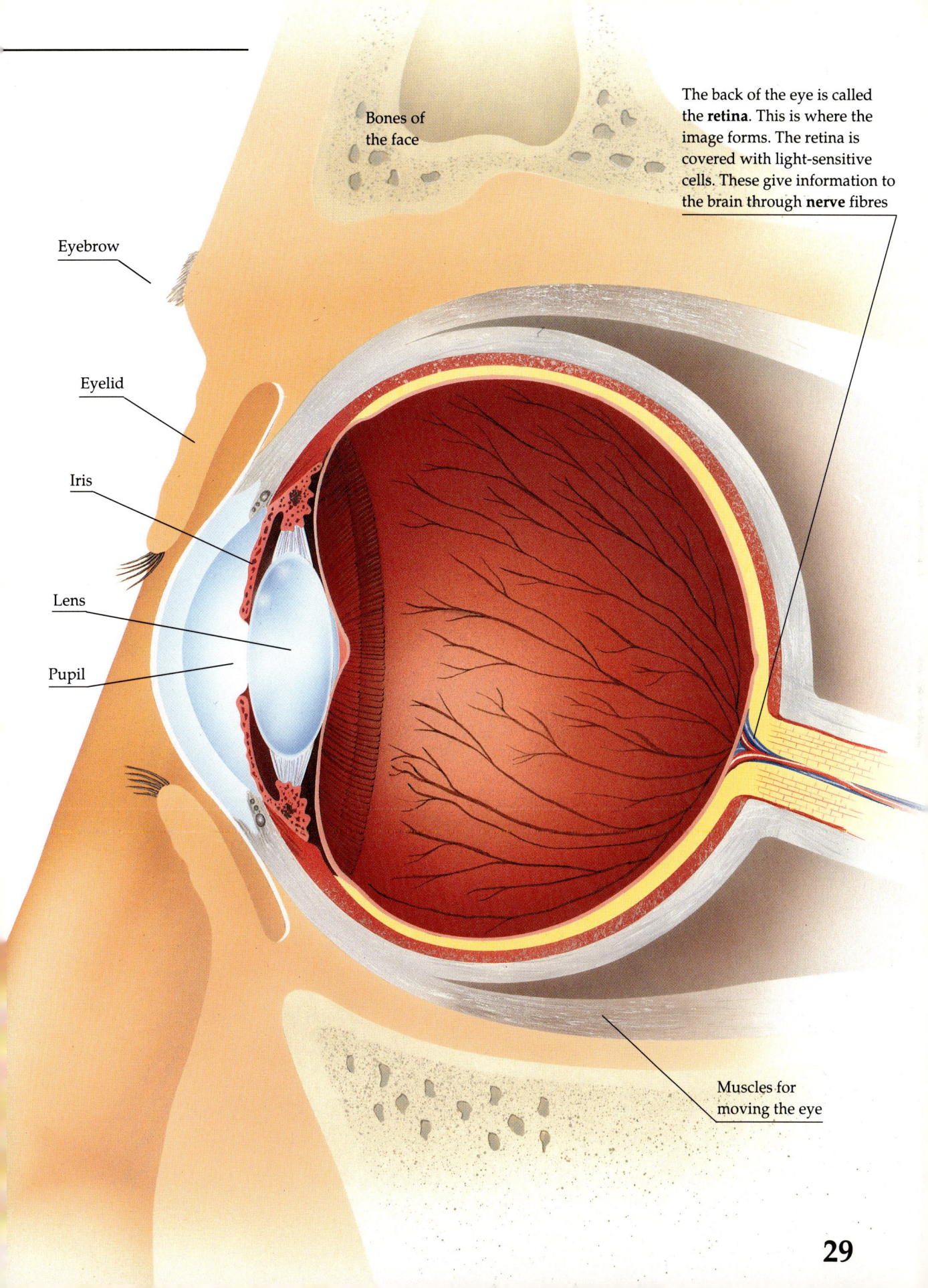

Capturing the Moon and stars

A telescope is used to make things appear close even though they are a long way away. You might use a telescope to look at a ship out at sea, or to look at the Moon and stars.

There are two ways of doing this. One is to use a lens, and the other is to use a dished mirror. The world's biggest telescopes big mirrors to gather the light and small lenses to focus it to an eyepiece. They are called reflecting telescopes.

Make a reflecting telescope
You can use a dished shaving mirror to make a telescope. You will also need a small flat mirror and a magnifying glass.

Set the shaving mirror so it faces the Moon. Move the small flat mirror in front of the dish until it bounces the light from the Moon towards you.

Look at the reflection with a magnifying glass and you see the Moon enlarged. You have made a reflecting telescope.

Path of light from space

Magnifying glass

Caution:
Never use the telescope to look at the Sun. It can cause blindness

Small flat (vanity) mirror

Shaving mirror

Observatories

Some of the world's largest lenses are used in telescopes to see the faint light that is millions and millions of kilometres away. Some telescopes are so big they have to be housed in special buildings called **observatories**.

The largest lens ever made for a telescope was for the Yerkes Observatory in the USA. It measures over one metre across.

The largest mirror used in a telescope is six metres across. It is housed in an observatory in the Caucasus region of the USSR. The mirror weighs an incredible 70 tonnes!

Star bursts

This picture is of a distant mass of dust and gas called a nebula. You can also see many stars. Notice that many of the stars are different in colour from our Sun.

The world turned upside down

Everything in our world seems the right way up. But when you look in some types of glass the world is turned upside down. Even looking through a small hole can turn the world upside down.

This is how you should hold your pin-hole camera. It is best if the rest of the room is dark and only the object brightly lit

Turn your world upside down
To make an upside down machine, or pin-hole camera, you need a cardboard tube. The one here is part of a tube that protected a poster.

Cut the tube to be about 10 centimetres long. Fasten a sheet of tracing paper over one end using a elastic band. This is the place where the image will form.

Fasten thick wrapping paper across the other end of the tube. Use a pencil to pierce a hole about as big as the pencil lead. This hole is going to turn your world upside down.

Hold the tube so that you can see the tracing paper screen and turn the tube until you can see a *very* well lit object such as a table lamp or a window with sunlight streaming through.

Lens

Winder

Camera back

Film holder

Shutter

Film goes
across here

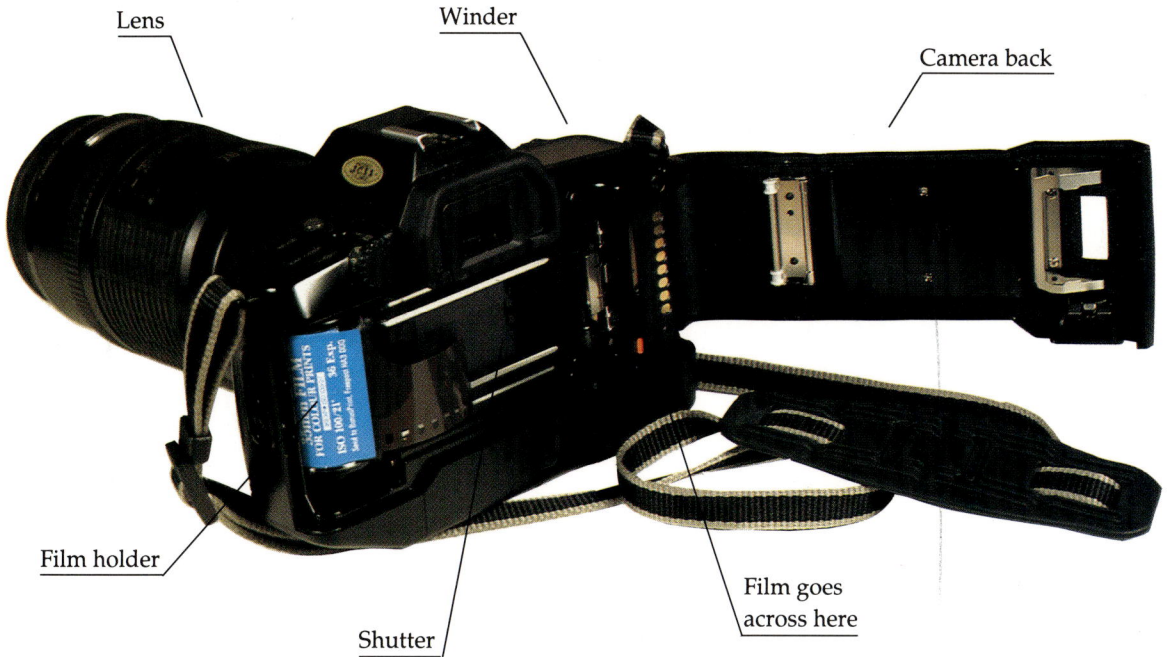

Modern cameras

Modern cameras have replaced the tiny pin hole
with a lens that will let in enough to produce an
image of even poorly lit objects. Nevertheless, the
way the modern camera works is basically the same
as for the pin-hole camera.

If you ask a grown-up to open a camera
and let you see the lens (tell them they
may have to set the camera to 'B'),
the view you get is still upside
down. You can put a sheet of
tracing paper across the back
and get an image in just the
same way as your pin
hole camera.

Tracing paper
and elastic bands

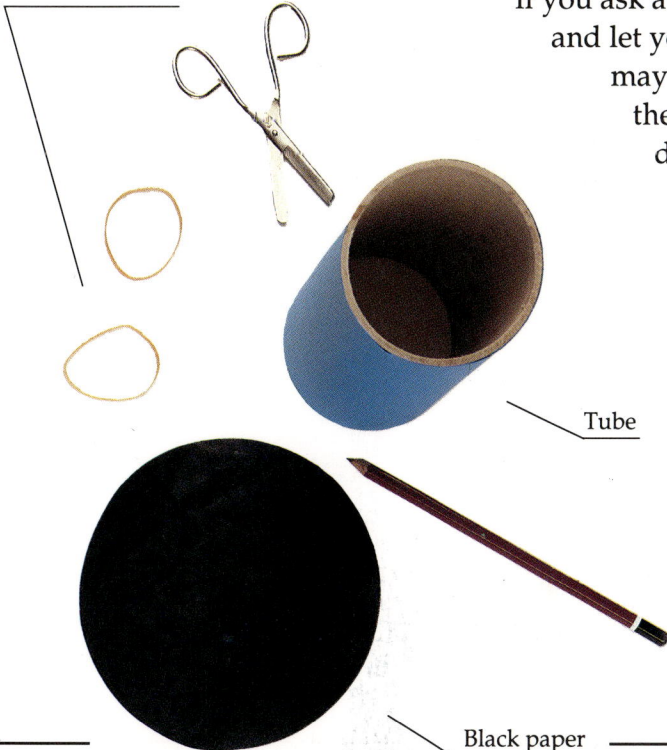

Tube

Black paper

Making rainbows

Rainbows are the brilliant arcs of coloured lights that often shine in the sky after it has rained. But rainbow effects are found in some surprising places. They occur on an oily road and even on the disks of your home CD player. Here is why they are so common.

A spectrum of light

The colours we see in a rainbow all existed in white light, but they were mixed together. Some natural transparent materials, such as the triangular glass prism shown below, or raindrops separate out the colours and spread them out so that we can see each colour side by side. This is called a **spectrum**.

Make rainbow effects

Put a drop of oil onto a saucer of water then look for the rainbow effect. Remember you will only see the rainbow when you look at it from the right angle, so you will have to experiment a bit.

A rainbow can also be produced using a dish of water and a small flat mirror. Choose a place lit by sunlight or a strong lamp. Dip a mirror into a dish of water, with the bottom edge inside the water and the top edge resting against the side of the dish. Change the angle of the mirror until you get a good rainbow effect reflected onto a nearby wall.

Surface effect

The surfaces of CDs are made in a special way that let them reflect the light just to give a spectrum.

Hold a CD in the light so you can see the rainbow. *Very carefully* turn the disc in different ways and you will see many interesting rainbow patterns.

Rainbows

Rain is made of many tiny droplets. Each droplet is ball-shaped and when light shines on it the light is reflected almost back on itself. You only see a rainbow when strong sunlight shines on falling rain or the spray from a waterfall like the one shown here.

Mixing colours

All the colours of the spectrum can be combined to make white light. But white light can also appear to be made from three special, or **primary, colours**. So by mixing primary colours in different proportions we can create all the colours of the rainbow easily.

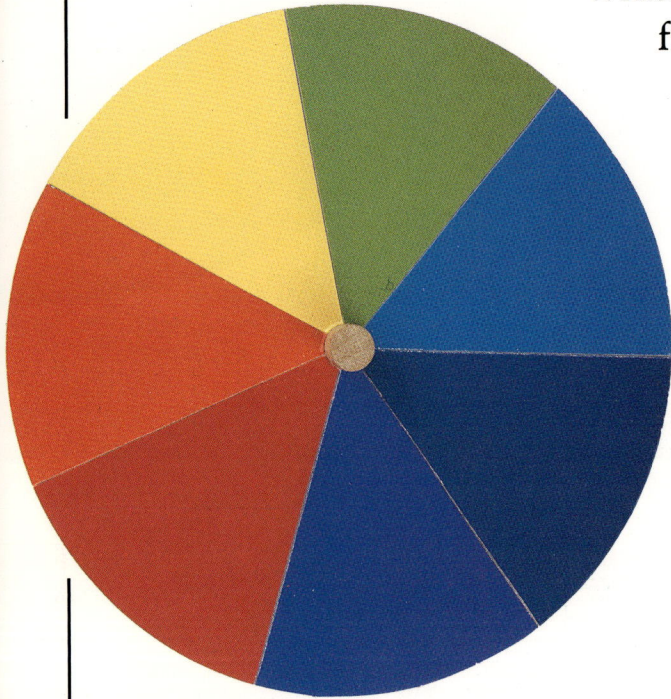

The colours we can see

When the Sun shines or we switch on a light bulb it sends out rays of many types. We can only see some of these rays: these are the visible rays that make up the spectrum.

On this disc are the seven colours of the visible spectrum in the order they are normally seen: red, orange, yellow, green, blue, indigo, and violet.

Making white light

It is easy to show that white light is made of the colours of the spectrum. To do this you need a piece of card, a sharp pencil and some coloured pencils. Trace off the disc shown here and transfer the shape onto a card. Colour each piece of the card and then cut out the disk. Push a pencil through the centre of the disc so that it is tightly gripped by the disc.

Spin the disc and you will see all the colours disappear, and be replaced by a near-white colour. This works because the brain has remembered all the colours and added them together.

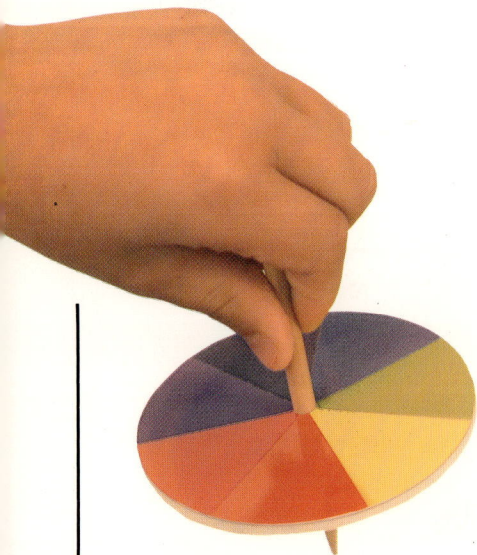

Primary colours

If you make up a spinner disk like the one shown on the right, you will see whitish light when you spin it.

This disk only has three colours on it: red, green and blue. These are the primary colours.

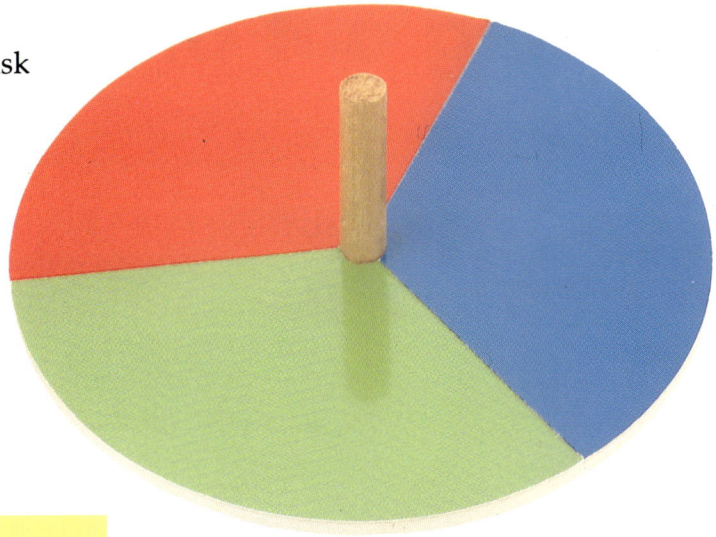

Make new colours

Make a spinner that is half green and half red and spin it. Then try half red and half blue and finally half blue and half green. One of them will look yellow, another will look a reddish colour called magenta and another will look a blue colour called cyan. Can you find which colour mix creates which new colour?

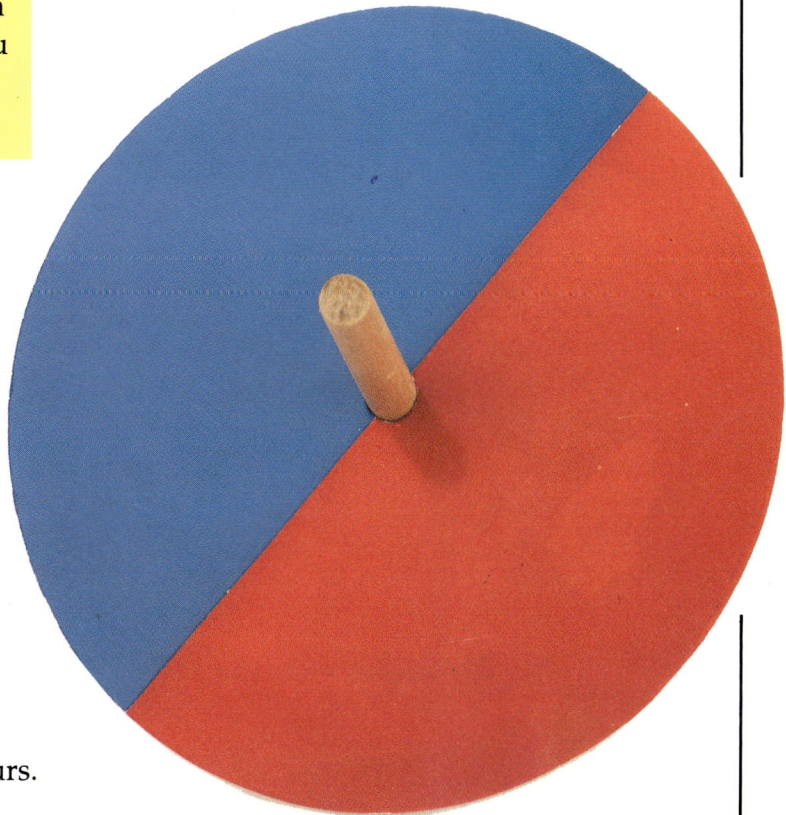

TV tricks

The three primary colours are used to give your television screen its colour.

Look closely at a colour television screen: you should be able to see tiny dots of red, green and blue. From a distance your eyes merge these dots to give a spectrum of colours.

Standing out and blending in

We see patterns of colour all the time.
Different colours help us to see objects.
Big contrasts in colour make an object
stand out. But things that have similar
colours are difficult to tell apart.
They blend in to the background.

Standing out

Sometimes it is very useful
to be seen clearly. This
macaw has bright colours
to help it to attract a mate
in the dark green tropical
rainforests where it lives.

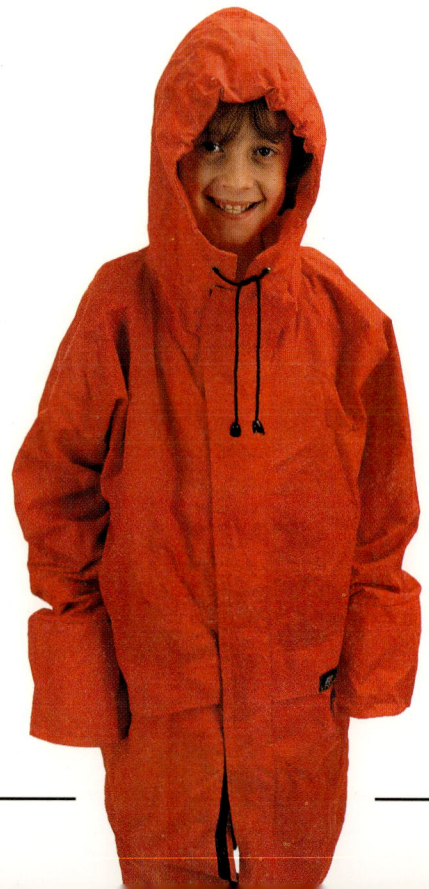

Be seen, be safe

It is especially important to be seen in dangerous situations. Many people who ride bicycles wear brightly coloured and reflective clothes so that they stand out in the headlights of a car. Walkers often wear brightly coloured protective clothes so that they can be spotted by rescue teams in case of emergency.

Camouflage

Sometimes you lose something and have difficulty finding it. The chances are it blends in so well with its surroundings that you can't easily spot it. It is **camouflaged**.

Pattern is a form of camouflage. The irregular shapes confuse the eye and make it difficult to see shapes properly.

Many creatures use camouflage for their survival. Some, like the reptile called the chameleon, can change colour to match their new surroundings. A deer, that has a dappled brown and white coat is hard to spot in the shady parts of the woods where it lives. A polar bear has white fur to make it harder for its prey to spot it.

Filtering through

Most coloured light starts off as white light. The colours are made by cutting out all the unwanted parts of the spectrum. Transparent materials that do this are called filters.

Filters

Filters are made from transparent coloured material. A red filter is used to allow only red light to shine through, a blue filter to allow only blue light to shine and so forth.

Each filter blocks out all other parts of the spectrum. So if you put two different coloured filters in front of each other no light gets through.

These filters are used in front of camera lenses to make special effects

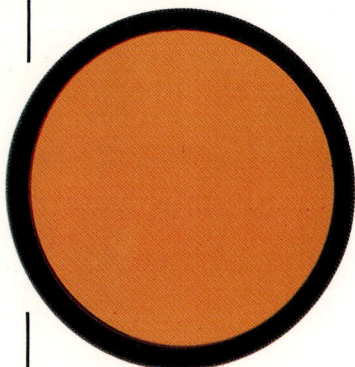

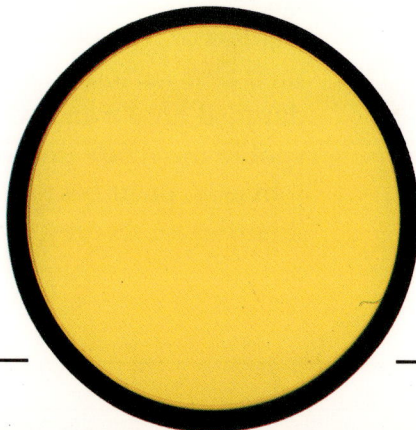

Special effects

Filters are often used in concerts to give special effects Here you can see two blue-filtered lights being uses as the main spotlights, with a red filtered light shining from above.

Glowing glass

The picture on the right shows a stained glass window from a church. Many tiny pieces of coloured glass have been placed together to make a pattern. When the light shines through the glass the picture shines brightly.

To make a 'stained glass window' using transparent coloured paper and card, first think up a design and make a drawing of it. Then transfer the drawing to a piece of stiff card. Next cut out the card, making holes where the 'stained glass' will be. Leave plenty of room for the coloured paper to be stuck to the frame.

Make your 'glass' from pieces of coloured transparent paper. Wrappings from sweets or painted tracing paper can also be used. Stick each piece over the card to complete your design and then hold it up to the light.

Piece of paper being stuck on to the back of the card

The finished window seen from the front

Strip of coloured transparent paper

41

Natural shadows

Light travels in straight lines. If light is blocked by an object it will throw a shadow just as these tree trunks cast a shadow on the ground.

Natural shadows change with the positions of the Sun, the Earth and the Moon.

Shadows and eclipses

Just as the trees cast a shadow on the ground, so the Earth casts a shadow on the Moon and sometimes the Moon casts a shadow on the Earth.

When the Moon comes between the Earth and the Sun the sky becomes dark. This is called an **eclipse** of the Sun and it is shown in the picture to the left.

When the Earth gets completely in the way of the Sun, no light reaches the Moon and you cannot see it. This is an eclipse of the Moon.

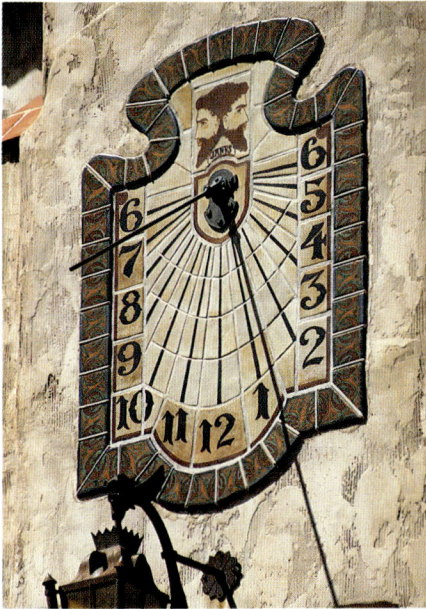

Shadow time

Since early times people have used shadows to tell the time. The instrument they made was called a Sun clock or Sundial. This picture shows a Sundial on a wall. If you want to make your own simple Sun clock all you need is a stick.

To set your Sun clock push the stick firmly into the ground in a spot that will not be shaded by trees or buildings. When your wrist-watch reaches the hour place a small stick or stone where the shadow of the stick falls. Label it with the hour. Leave the stick in place and come back to mark the shadow for each hour during the day.

The Moon's phases

How much of the Moon we see depends on shadows. For most of the time we see a crescent shaped Moon. The size of the crescent changes as the Moon circles the Earth. A fairly 'new' Moon is a small crescent. The sky is very dark on such nights. A full Moon occurs when we can see the whole of the sunlit Moon. This gives bright nights. The different shapes of crescent are called the phases of the Moon.

Playing with shadows

Shadows are cast when an **opaque** object blocks a beam of light. Because light travels in straight lines, the shadow has clear outlines. The size of the shadow depends on the distance between the light, the object and the surface on which the shadow falls.

People have used the idea of changing sizes of shadows for centuries in their shadow plays.

Javanese puppet master
This is a shadow puppet from the Indonesian island of Java. Notice that the puppet-maker has taken the trouble to paint the puppet even though it is only seen as a shadow. In Java each puppet represents a special character in their traditional stories. Many countries have traditional puppets like these.

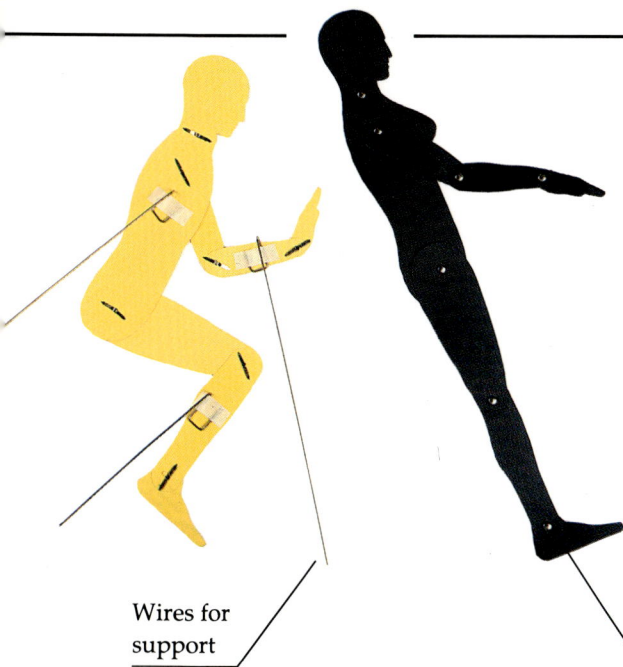

Make shadow puppets

To make your own shadow play you need to make up a story. Then you cut out the main characters in paper, making each one into an easily seen outline. Glue each paper shape on to a stick. You are now ready to make a shadow play

In a darkened room use a single light. The narrow beam of light from a slide projector is best of all. Arrange for the light to cast shadows on a plain wall.

Wires for support

Joints made from paper fasteners

Begin your play by pushing each character into the light. Use the sticks to make them pop up from beneath the light. You can decide how big each shadow should be by choosing the distances between puppets, wall and lamp. Try out a few different distances until you get the best effect. You may want to have giant shadows. For this you need the puppets close to the light. You may want the puppets to grow (like a genie) or shrink (like Alice in Wonderland). To get this effect just move the puppets closer or farther from the light.

Copy some of these shadows to make you puppets, then make some more to your own designs.

What the audience sees

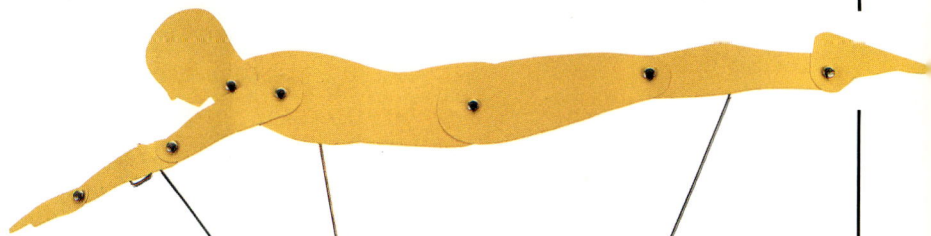

How the puppets are held

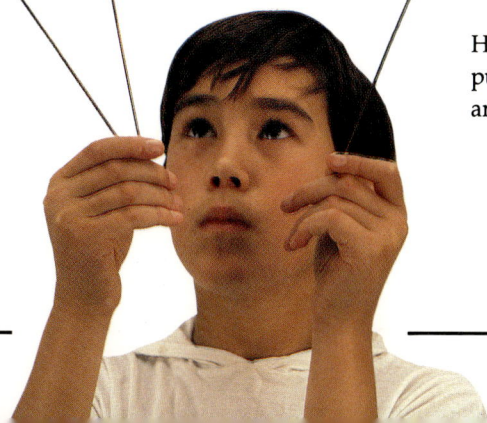

New words

atmosphere
the layer of gases around the Earth. The lowest part of the atmosphere includes enough oxygen for us to breath. It also holds large amounts of dust and other tiny particles that have been swept off the land by winds

camouflage
the way in which objects can be difficult to see because they so closely resemble their surroundings. Most types of camouflage involve patterns of colours, such as stripes or blotches

concave
the way a surface is dished so that it faces inwards. Typical concave objects include the inside of a spoon and the inside of a cupped hand

convex
the way a surface is bulged out so that it faces outwards. The outside of a ball is a convex surface

eclipse
an eclipse occurs when one planet or Moon shuts out the direct sunlight to another. In an eclipse of the Sun, the Moon passes between the Sun and the Earth, almost blocking it out for several minutes

energy
the property of light waves that plants can use to grow

fluorescent
a special property of some materials such that they give off light which we can see when they are put in a beam of light rays outside our normal range of vision

image
when light rays are bounced off a mirror, or bent through a lens, they show a picture of the objects they 'see'. This picture is called an image

incandescent
the light that is produced when a solid, such as a wire in a lamp, is heated

kaleidoscope
the name given to a toy that uses several mirrors all facing inwards. The kaleidoscope produces many images of any object placed inside and this may give many new patterns

lens
when light passes through any transparent object that has curved sides the rays of light will be bent. The curved material is then a lens

light
a special form of energy that can be seen. Light energy can travel through space, which is why the Sun can still give energy to our world even though the Sun and Earth are over 150 million kilometres apart

mirror
most mirrors are made of glass with a layer of silver painted on to the back to give the reflecting surface

nerve
cord-like bundles of fibres that carry messages around the body. The nerves that connect the eye to the brain are often called the optical nerves

observatory
a place for the scientific study of space. The world's largest optical observatories are placed on high mountains well away from the pollution of cities so they can get the clearest possible view of space

opaque
a material which appears solid and which cannot be seen through. Most objects are opaque

periscope
a device for reflecting light through two right angles. This makes it possible for an observer to see over obstacles or round corners

primary colours
the minimum number of colours that, when mixed in the right proportions, can give all the other colours of the spectrum. They are usually red, green and blue

prism
a triangular-shaped piece of glass which is used to reflect light. One special property of prisms is to show that white light is really made up of many colours

pupil
the dark centre to the eye. The size of the pupil is controlled by changes in the iris, the coloured part of the eye

quartz
this is a common mineral that makes sand and glass. In its crystal form it is transparent

ray
the path followed by light as it moves from its source. Light can be made into rays by putting an obstruction, such as a comb, in front of a beam of light

rectangular
a shape that has square corners. A square is a special kind of rectangle where all the sides are the same length

retina
the part of the eye on which image is formed after light has passed through the lens. There are millions of tiny light-sensitive cells on the retina surface. Each is connected through a nerve directly to the brain

spectrum
the range of colours that make up white light

transparent
a material which will allow light to pass through it. Glass and water are examples of transparent materials

Index